GIS Guidebook:

GIS Automation with ModelBuilder

for ArcGIS Pro

By David W. Allen, GISP

GIS Guidebooks Publishing

Published by GIS Guidebooks Publishing

Www.GISGuidebooks.com

Corsicana, TX

info@GISGuidebooks.com

ISBN-13: 978-0-578-36053-9

www.ingramcontent.com/pod-product-compliance
Lightning Source LLC
Chambersburg PA
CBHW042125070326
40689CB00046B/613

About the Author

David Allen has been working with GIS since 1983, developed the GIS implementation for the City of Euless and has worked there over 30 years, taught evening classes in the GIS program at Tarrant County College for almost 20 years, and has published many other bestselling books on GIS. He knows this stuff inside and out … and he has a great knack at being able to explain complex topics in a simple way. He has been working with ArcGIS Pro since the first Beta, has traveled to Redlands many times to work with the developers and test these new tools, and is continually working on new methods and ideas of how this stuff can be put to best use.

Gis Guidebook:
GIS Automation with ModelBuilder for ArcGIS Pro

Table of Contents

Author's Introduction

ModelBuilder has been around for a long time, making it's debut in ArcMap as a quick way to string a few geoprocessing tools together. Then it got a revamp and a lot of new tools were added that let you set variables and control the flow of the processes so that things didn't necessarily have to be a linear path. Now with ArcGIS Pro, even more tools have been added to make it a pretty powerful way to automate your GIS processes. You'll find a host of what they call model-only tools that only work inside of a model, making it even more important to know what these tools are and how to configure them.

ModelBuilder has lots of online documentation to show you what tools are available, and tutorials that show you what the tools do. But what they don't do, and what this book tries to do, is show you how to link all these tools together to make fully functional, automated processes - start to finish. This isn't about just feeding a layer into a buffer and thinking that's automation, this is about setting up a user interface to get input parameters, processing data, making decisions on what tools need to be run and how they are configured, and getting a usable output. Some models might be ones you write and run once because of the complexity of the process, or ones that you write and use over and over, or even share with others to make your data processing easier.

Also, the data used here is totally and completely irrelevant. Please don't get hung up on the idea that some polygons represent a certain type of data or that some points represent data that you have no interest in. They are all points, lines, and polygons. If you don't like the idea of working with lemonade stand locations in census tracts, pretend that they are temperature sensing stations in lava fields. It doesn't matter, they're still just points and polygons. When you complete an exercise you might want to find some of your own data that is similar and try to replicate the lesson. It would be good practice! You might even try a different approach or even different tools. You know what they say about programming: It doesn't matter if the journey is short or long; people marvel at the result.

It is expected that you already know how to use ArcGIS Pro and work with project files before starting this book. No instruction will be given on how to open project documents, how to access menu tools, how to navigate through control panes, etc ... If you are not comfortable working in ArcGIS Pro then I would suggest starting with a book on that topic.

Throughout the book you will also see "Rafael's Question", which is a question students typically ask in the classroom except in this situation I have to both ask and answer them. You will also find "Rafael's Challenge" throughout the book. There is also a document you can download with extra challenges where you will take techniques you've learned and apply them to models with minimal instruction. Helpful tips are given that you can reference as you solve the dilemmas.

Dig in, have fun, and learn to build great models!

DWA

The exercise data and materials can be found and downloaded at

http://GISGuidebooks.com/ModelBuilder

Introduction to Building Models

ArcGIS Pro has a special graphically oriented programming tool built in that's called ModelBuilder. This tool will let you automate a workflow by dragging geoprocessing tools, python scripts, and other items into an interface and linking them together. Then when the model is run the tools will execute in the order that you design. It can be very helpful in automating a task that you repeat often, automating a complex task that others need to run, or even documenting a workflow that you may not do often enough to remember all the details. Whatever your purpose, you'll find that models can be a great help in your GIS data processing.

Basic Model Components

Models are stored in toolboxes, and these can be the default toolbox that is created with every project, or custom toolboxes that you make yourself. From the toolbox you can create, edit, or run the models.

Note that since models are stored in a toolbox, they are for the current project only and do not carry over from one project to the next. You can, however, export toolboxes and the models they contain for use by others but remember that the other projects would have to contain the same data in order for the models to function correctly. Also, if you package a project the toolbox and the models it may contain are part of the package.

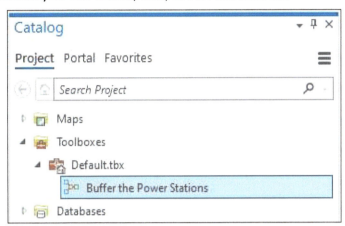

Models contain components that represent the workflow consisting of a geoprocessing tool, one or more inputs for the tool, and the output of the tool.

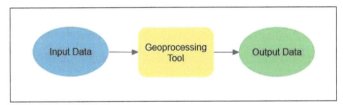

The geoprocessing tools are represented by a yellow box, the inputs by a blue box, and the outputs by a green box. The lines show which elements are connected to what, and in what direction the model is flowing.

A single input may be used for several geoprocessing tools. This is done simply by drawing a connecting arrow to multiple tools. The tools may be different and will each create a different output.

More importantly, however, is that the output of one model process can be used as the input for another process.

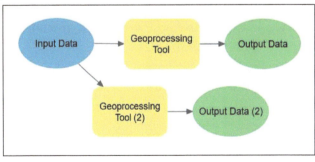

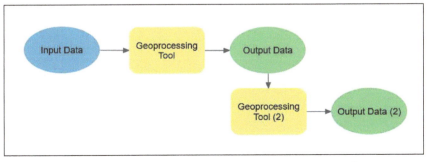

Any number of process can be strung together to represent the workflow providing that the outputs are of the correct type of data for the next input.

Models should follow your logical workflow and line up the processes in sequence. In fact, when a model runs it will change the color of the processes to show which tool is running and in what order. The yellow boxes will turn red for the active tool, then change back when the tool completes and the next tool runs.

The model components can also indicate what run state they are in. This can help you to make sure that your model is ready and capable of running before you execute it. A model that is not fully ready to run will not produce any results.

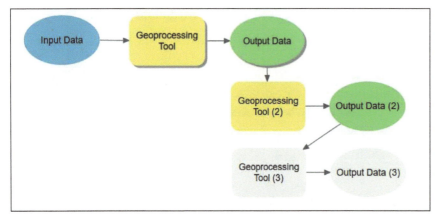

In this image, the geoprocessing tool with the gray drop shadow is in the "Has Been Run" state. The geoprocessing too that is yellow but has no drop shadow is in the "Ready to Run" state. The gray geoprocessing tool is in the "Not Ready to Run" state, which occurs when the tool is not fullly configured. These can be a great help when you are designing and troubleshooting your models.

Rafael's Question: *Seems pretty simple so far, but wouldn't that just repeat the same process over and over without change and keep making the same datasets?*
First, it really is that simple. And secondly, there are a LOT of more complex items we'll be adding to the models to let you change the workflow to match different scenarios ... and that's what this book is for!

Exercise 1 – Watch a model in action

For this exercise it would be helpful to see a completed model and watch it run. First examine the model and notice what the workflow is designed to do. The model selects a subset of transmission tower features from a layer, then buffers those towers. Next notice that the tools will turn red as they run, and they move from the "Ready to Run" state to the "Has Been Run" state.
** *if you have not done so, go download the book materials: http://GISGuidebooks.com/ModelBuilder* **

1 **Navigate to the folder where you installed the class materials, then open the folder /Projects/Exercise 1/.**

2 **View the video Sample Model Video.**

If you would like to see this model in person, it is set up to run in the included project folder.

3 **Open the ArcGIS Pro project file Exercise 1.**

The model is already open and in the "Not Ready to Run" state.

4 **Run the model by clicking the Run button on the toolbar.**

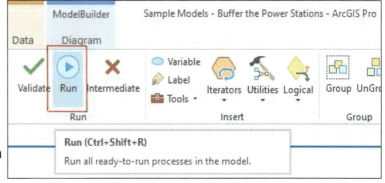

Watch carefully because the processing happens much faster than what is displayed in the video. The selection tool runs first to select all the transmission towers that meet the criteria, then the buffer tool runs and creates a new output feature class. This process can be repeated over and over, ensuring that the results are consistent each time.

If you like, you can move to the Map pane and examine the output file that was generated.

5 **Close ArcGIS Pro.**

As you saw in that exercise, there is a separate editing window called the Model Canvas; a graphic interface in which all the tools and data are brought together and connected into a process. There are many ways to add tools and data to the model canvas. The easiest is to drag a tool from the Geoprocessing Pane, and drag data from the Contents pane. You may also add tools and some of the model-only features from the menu bar, or add these items from the context menu. And one of the simplest ways to add tools is to place the cursor in the model canvas and just start typing the name of a geoprocessing tool. A search window will open and help you find the correct tool. One word of caution, though, is that when using this technique you must type the tool's name using only lower case letters (there's a long reason for this).

Once items are added to the model canvas the connections are made just by drawing lines between them. Tools are configured by opening their dialogs, which will be the same as if you had run the tool from the Geoprocessing pane, so this will look very familiar.

Exercise 2 – Adding and configuring Model Elements

In this exercise you'll see how tools and data are added, connected, and configured in a rather simple model. The model will take an input polygon and use it to clip data from a larger dataset. The input will be the county boundary for Navarro County, Texas, and the features to be clipped are the railroad lines for the entire state of Texas.

1 **Open Exercise 2 from the Project folder in the book materials.**

A model called Clip Railroads for Navarro County 1 has already been created and the model canvas is open. In the contents pane you'll see the Railways and Navarro County layers needed for this process.

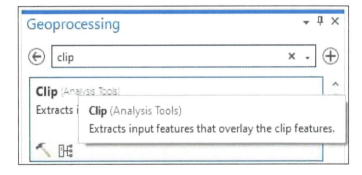

2 **On the right side of the screen, click the Geoprocessing pane and search for the Clip tool.**

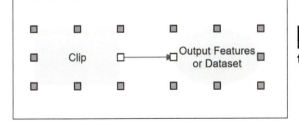

3 **Click and hold on the tool, then drag it to the center of the model canvas.**

The tool comes in as two elements - a gray shaded rectangle (representing the tool) and a gray shaded oval (representing the output). The color means that they have not yet been configured, and the model will not run until the tools are properly configured.

4 Find the Railways layer in the Contents pane and drag it into the model canvas to a spot just left of the Clip tool. Then drag the Navarro County layer into the model canvas and place it just below the other layer.

Word of caution: the model canvas is very sensitive about selecting, moving, and connecting elements. If you see an element with the "drag ears" around it (all the little boxes) it means that the element is currently "selected" and you can only resize or move it, not configure it. You may have several elements selected to resize or move, but you have to click in a blank area of the canvas to "unselect" them in order to link elements or open their configuration window.

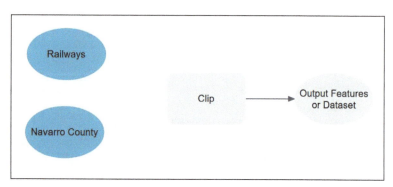

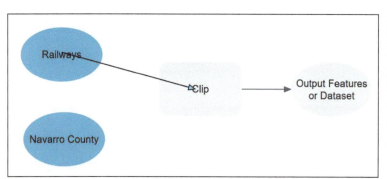

5 Click in an empty area to ensure that none of the elements are selected.

6 Click and hold on the Railways element and draw a line from it to the Clip element and release the mouse button. You'll see a directional arrow being drawn.

7 After you let up, a configuration box will appear prompting you to select the role this data will play in the Clip function. Click on Input Features.

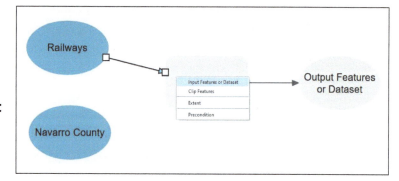

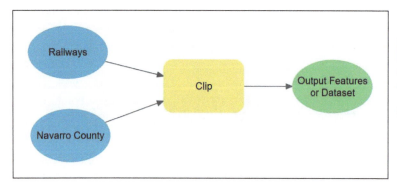

8 Repeat the process with the Navarro County element and make it the Clip Feature. The model will move to the Ready-To-Run state.

Technically, it would run but you don't know what the name of the output features would be, or where they would be stored. There's two ways to find out, though. The first is to just hover the mouse over the tool and a pop-up window will display the tool's parameters.

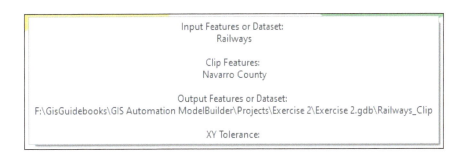

9 Hover the mouse over the yellow Clip tool.

You can see that the output is being saved to the default project folder using a default name. To change that you can open the tool's parameter dialog box and it will display the same window that the tool would display if you were running it directly from the Geoprocessing pane.

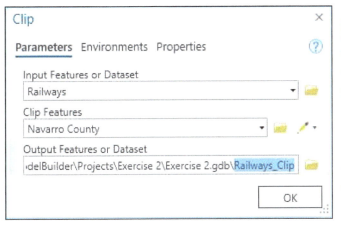

10 Double click the yellow Clip tool. You'll see the default output location and name which you could change, but for this exercise leave it at the default setting and click OK.

That's all there is to this model, but for fun you will look at other ways to add the tools and make the element connections.

In the ModelBuilder menu bar across the top of the screen you will see a panel called Insert. It's more commonly used to add model-specific components that can't be found elsewhere, but it also includes a drop-down window that will let you search for and add tools to your model. Once opened the window will find tools exactly the same way as the Geoprocessing Pane.

11 In the ModelBuilder menu, click Save.

12 Click and move to the display window Clip Railroads for Navarro County – 2 to get an empty Model Canvas.

13 In the main menu, find the Insert panel and click the down-arrow next to Tools.

14 Type Clip in the resulting search tool.

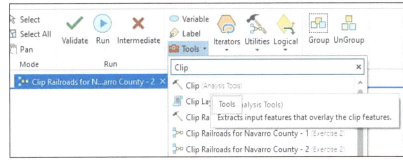

Rafael's Question – *Why do I see two tools with the same names as the models I'm writing?*
When you make a model, it becomes a geoprocessing tool and is available on all geoprocessing tool searches. The software, however, doesn't know that you haven't configured the model yet. Notice also that it has a different icon – one that looks like the colored elements in a model. That lets you know that this is a model and not a system tool (which has a hammer icon). You may also see a tool icon that looks like a scroll of paper, which tells you that it is a custom script.

15 Select the Clip (Analysis) tool and drag it into the model canvas. It appears in the Not-Ready-To-Run state.

You know that the clip tool requires two input, the features to be clipped and the features to do the clipping. To get them into the model and added tot he tool's parameter, you can just drag the layer from the Contents pane and drop them directly on top of the tool. Then a configuration window will open and prompt you to define the layer's role in the process.

16 Select the Railways layer in the Contents pane and drag it into the model canvas, dropping it on top of the Clip tool.

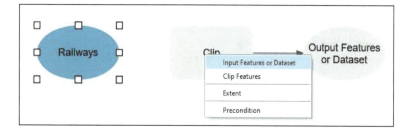

17 Select Input Features or Dataset to finish the configuration.

The data layer drops right into the model and the connection arrow is automatically drawn.

18 Repeat the action with the Navarro County layer, setting it as the Clip Features.

Note: There's one quirk with this – the second layer will be placed directly on top of the first layer, but you can select it and drag it to a new location.

That worked pretty well and went pretty quickly, but there's another way to do this that you might find even faster. It involves using the model canvas search to get the tools and the configuration window to find and add data layers.

19 In the ModelBuilder menu, click Save.

20 Move to the display window Clip Railroads for Navarro County – 3 to get a new, blank model canvas.

21 Click the mouse anywhere in the model canvas to make sure the window is active. Then start typing the name of the tool you want ... clip.

Note: There's a quirk here, too. Because there are shortcut keys used throughout ArcGIS Pro which use capital letters, you have to type the tool names in lower case letters. If your search looked for tools starting with an I, start over using a lower case c.

22 Select the Clip (Analysis) tool and drag it into the model canvas (you could also just double click it).

23 Next, double click the Clip tool to open the configuration window.

24 Use the drop-down arrows to set the Input and Clip features. Then click OK.

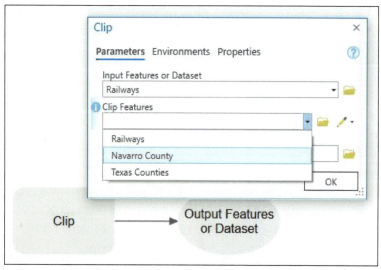

Poof – the tool is configured and the two layers you selected are automatically added to the model. Note also that the tool becomes colorized to the Ready-To-Run state.

25 **Click Save in the ModelBuilder menu, then save the project. If you are not continuing, close the project.**

The ModelBuilder Menu

Now that you've seen how models work and gotten some experience adding and configuring tools, you'll look at how to create a new model and investigate some of the model canvas tools.

There are a lot of items on the ModelBuilder menu. Some are pretty self explanatory and resemble buttons and tools that are common to most menus. Items like cutting, copying, or pasting model elements look just like any other program. And things like starting a new model, saving the existing model, or exporting the model are pretty common. There are also some View tools to manage how the model canvas is displayed, like zooming and adjusting the display area. See how many of these you recognize.

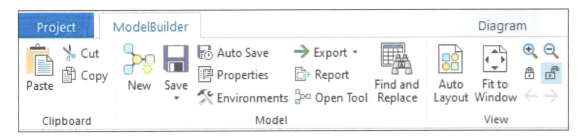

The other part of the ModelBuilder menu has tools that let you interact with the model. This may include selecting and moving elements, running or testing the model, adding geoprocessing tools or model-specific elements, and grouping or organizing the elements in the model canvas. More of how these tools are used will be covered later on.

Note that Undo/Redo on the main menu will affect any of the things you do in ModelBuilder, so if you try the Auto Layout and don't like the results, you can Undo.

Exercise 3 – Using the Menu and the Model Canvas

In this exercise you'll use some of the features of the model menu to interact with the elements in the model canvas.

1 **Open the project Exercise 3.**

The project already has a model, called Model, that does some processing on the freeway and street data. It is the basis for a much more complex model that the designer wants to build.

2 **Open the model named Model if it isn't open already.**

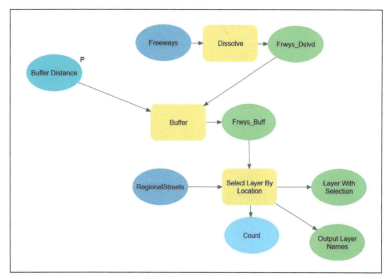

Right now it looks like a mess. For one, the name isn't very descriptive, and if you make a new model, ArcGIS Pro will name it Model as well. These things have to have a descriptive name. Think of it as if you are designing your own geoprocessing tool and you want others to be able to search for it in the tool box, and name it accordingly. This is done through the model properties.

3 **In the Model area of the menu, click on Properties. The Properties dialog box opens.**

4 **Change the name of the model to *MakeCommercialZones*. Change the Label to *Define Freeway Commercial Zone*. Add a description as shown and click OK.**

Model names do not allow spaces or special characters, so be careful with your values.

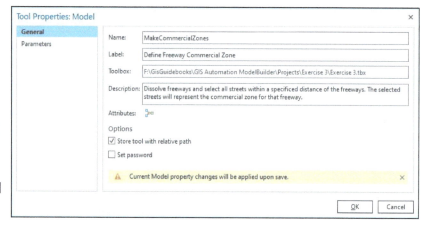

There's an interesting note at the bottom of this dialog. It's telling you that the name changes will not take place until the model is saved. Merely clicking OK won't do it.

5 **On the Model menu, click Save.**

The name of the model will change in both the window header and the Toolbox.
Next you will group some of the tools together to both make them easier to move around the canvas and to also identify what they do. You start by selecting the model elements with the Select tool.

6 **In the Model area of the menu click on the Select tool.**

7 **Select the three elements associated with the dissolve tool: Freeways, Dissolve, and Frwy_Dslvd. You can select them one by one while holding Shift, or drag a box across the three elements.**

8 **In the Group menu area, click Group.**

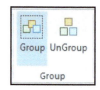

You'll see that the selected tools are placed in a yellow box with a title. Note that the functions of the tools or the order in which they run is not altered. The generic name of Group isn't very descriptive, so that should be changed.

9 Right click on the Group name and select Rename. Call the group Dissolve Freeways.

Ungroup – Returns the model elements to a free-standing position

Save as Model – creates a new model using just the elements in the group

Auto Layout Group – automatically rearranges the elements in the group to be more compact

Route Group Links – realigns the route lines between the group's elements

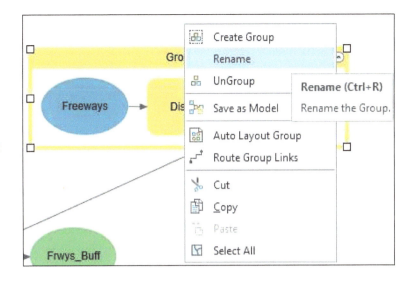

Experiment with these if you like but note that they only act upon the elements in the selected group.

10 With the Dissolve Freeways group still selected. Move the group to the top center of the model canvas.

Groups (and all the elements they contain) move as one piece, making it easier to organize your model.

You can also minimize a group (which makes the name even more important in identifying what the grouped elements do) and hovering the mouse over a group will reveal information about what the group contains.

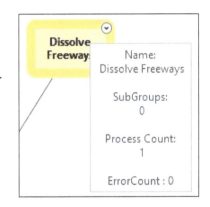

11 Make a group out of the three elements involved with the Buffer tool and rename it to Buffer Freeways. Then minimize the group.

Another item that is used to make your model more concise and informative is the addition of labels to the model canvas. One type of label is static within the model, moving only when you select it. The other type is tied to a model element and will move when that model element is moved. For practice you'll make one of each.

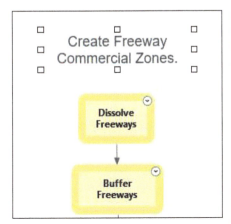

12 On the ModelBuilder menu in the Insert area, click on Label. Drag the new label element to the top of the model canvas. Right click it and select Rename, then name it 'Create Freeway Commercial Zones'. You can resize the label so that all the text is displayed.

This label will remain where it is, even if you move other elements around. The other type of label is tied to an element and created from the element's context menu.

13 Right click on the Layer With Selection element and select Create Label. Then right click the label and rename it to Selected Commercial Zones. You may need to resize the label so that all of the text is visible.

14 Select the Layer With Selection element and drag it to a new location. Note that the label moves with it.

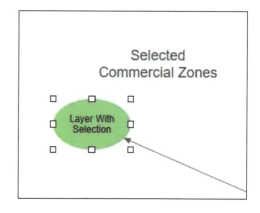

These labels don't have any real effect on the model other than to add documentation, however next time you edit a model you wrote more than a year ago you'll appreciate them even more.

You've seen many of the more common tools on the ModelBuilder toolbar, and now for the most controversial ... the Auto Layout tool. The intent of this tool is to automatically arrange the model elements in a logical and pleasing configuration, but in past it's been more of a nuisance that a blessing. The Esri programmers try to update it so that it does a better job but most people hate it. To ease the pain and make it a bit more useful, they have added two things ... the Auto Layout operation can be undone with the Undo button, and users have the ability to lock elements so that the Auto Layout tool can't move them. The next few steps will have you try these, and you can decide if you will embrace the Auto Layout in the future.

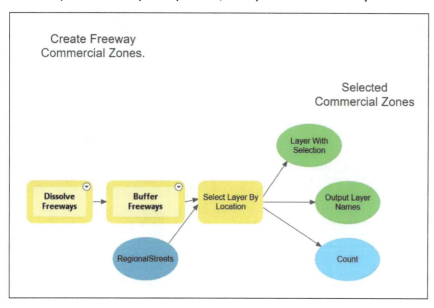

15 Save your model (in case something goes wrong).

16 In the View area of the ModelBuilder menu, click the Auto Layout tool.

You can see that the process moved everything around and tried to make a more organized layout. Do you love it or hate it? Imagine if you have a very large and complex model and clicked this tool and it repositions everything. You opinion might change!

Next try locking some of the elements and see if the results are more acceptable.

17 Click Undo (or type Ctrl-Z) to reset the model to it's prior layout.

18 Select the two groups you made along with the label at the top of the model canvas. In the View area of the menu, click Lock Element.

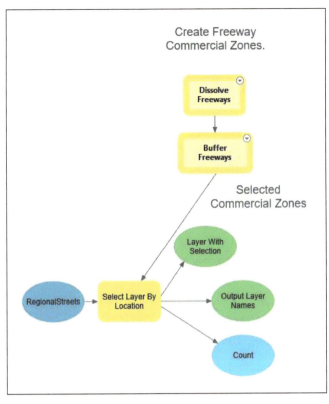

Create Freeway
Commercial Zones.

19 Again, click the Auto Layout tool. Click Fit to Window and examine the results.

Did you like this better or worse? You can decide in future your relationship with the Auto Layout tool.

20 Save the model and close the project.

At this point you should have a grasp on what it takes to create a new model, add tools, place labels, and arrange the elements in a manner of your choosing. Practice these fundamentals on every model you make because they will make your life easier when you (or co-workers) have to go back and try to understand what a model is doing.

Designing Functioning Models

Now that you are familiar with the basics, it's time to start making models that actually do something useful. For the rest of the book you'll be presented with a scenario and some datasets for a model project, then you will create and run a model that will solve the problem by following the exercise instructions.

In addition, you'll have an opportunity to create other models for the scenario or using similar techniques. Included with the downloaded materials is a document called Rafael's Challenges that is indexed by exercise with ideas for other models. Working through these will give you the maximum amount of hands-on experience with ModelBuilder. Note that in some cases there may be other ways to accomplish the goal of a particular scenario, but keep in mind that the object here is to practice using all the tools. If you see a different way to complete a model, go ahead and work through the exercise instructions, then build the model a second time to try out your ideas. Either way it'll be good practice with the model tools.

The first models that you will create use standard geoprocessing tools without any additional "model-only" tools. You can practice connecting tools and variables together as well as grouping and labeling elements. One of the simplest and easiest tools to understand is the buffer tool, so the exercise will start with that. Just remember that the tools and data here aren't the focus. Instead pay attention to the way the tools are combined and used in the model area to build custom geoprocessing tools.

Exercise 4 – Design a simple model

In this scenario you have some land parcels and water well locations. You will develop a model that will buffer the selected well site by a half mile, select all of the parcels that fall within the well buffer, and create an output file that can be used to send notices to the properties.

It's always a good idea to try working through the analysis steps manually first to make sure your process is correct. Models aren't that difficult to make, but they can be hard if you are inventing the process on-the-fly.

The steps for this analysis are:
- *Select a well site (point)*
- *Buffer the point by 2,640 feet (polygon)*
- *Overlay the buffer polygon on the land parcels (polygons) to select the parcels that intersect the buffer*
- *Create an Excel file with the results of the selection*

1 **Following the guidelines above, create a list of the geoprocessing tools you would use to accomplish this analysis, and note which files would be used as input for each tool. Then check your choices with the ones shown below.**

One answer is shown here -
- *User selects a well*
- *Buffer (Input Features is Water Wells, provide an output name, Distance is 2640)*
- *Select Layer by Location (Input Features is Land Parcels, Relationship is Intersects, Selecting Features is your new buffer file)*
- *Table to Excel (Input Table is Land Parcels, provide a name for the output Excel file)*

Remember that geoprocessing tools will only act upon the selected features (if there are any) so rest assured that the Buffer and Excel to Table tools will not try to work on the entire datasets.

Did you get a different answer? If so, work through the suggestions here, then afterwards you can go back and work the exercise a second time using your own process.

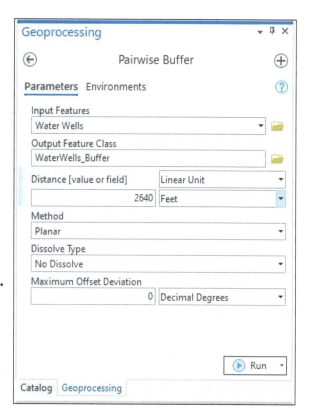

2 **Open the project Exercise 4 from the class materials.**

3 **Use the bookmark Mountain City to zoom to the area of interest.**

4 **Select one of the well sites.**

5 **In the Geoprocessing pane, locate and run the Buffer tool. Set the input to Water Wells, the output to WaterWells_Buffer, and the distance to 2460 feet. Click Run.**

6 Locate and run the Select Layer by Location tool. Set the input to Land Parcels – Hays County and the selecting features to WaterWells_Buffer. Click OK.

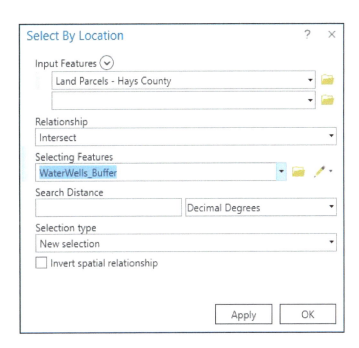

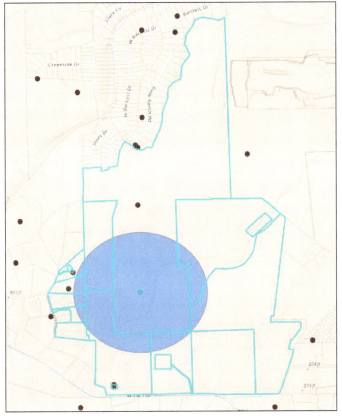

At this point you should have a set of selected parcels that fell within the specified distance of the well location. Something like this:

<----------------------------------

7 Next, locate the Table to Excel tool. Set the input to Land Parcels – Hays County and the output to PropertyList_Wells.xlsx (stored in the project's default folder). Click Run.

A few things to note along the way – The example used the Pairwise Buffer Tool. There is no difference between this and the standard buffer tool unless you are creating hundreds of buffers. The Pairwise tools examine the processing load required to complete and shunt this to multiple cores in your processor to accomplish the task very quickly. If you are doing one buffer it won't make any difference.

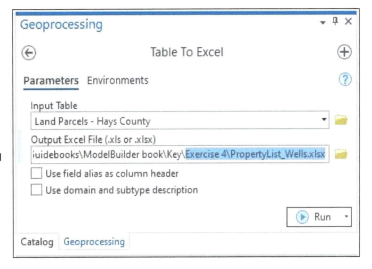

Also, the Table to Excel tool can produce both a .XLSX and a .XLS file. The file type is specified by manually adding the desired extension to the output file name.

The process seems to work and the results look great! If you had to do this many times a day, you would certainly want to try and automate the process. The parameters of all these geoprocessing tools will remain the same in the model so it should be easy to make the model.

First you need to actually create the model, and remember the importance of giving it a descriptive name and an appropriate description and tags.

8 In the Catalog pane, expand Toolboxes and right click on the toolbox Exercise 4.tbx. Select New > Model.

A new model is created called Model, and the model canvas is opened. You should remember how to rename it.

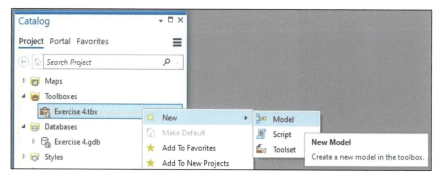

9 Rename the model to Well Property Selection and write an appropriate description. Click OK and save the model when done.

Next you'll need to add all the tools into the model in the same order and with the same parameters as when you ran them manually. There's an easy trick to this. Since you have previously run the tools with the correct parameters, you can drag in the tools from the geoprocessing history and they will already be configured.

10 In the Geoprocessing pane, click the green check mark next to Table to Excel and select Open History.

11 From the History pane, drag the (Pairwise) Buffer tool onto the model canvas.

12 Next drag the Select Layer By Location tool, followed by the Table to Excel tool.

Note how the tools drop in pre-configured, already connected, and Ready To Run.

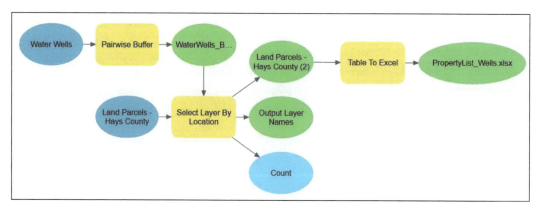

13 Save the model.

14 Move to the Map view and select a different well location.

15 Move back to the ModelBuilder pane and click Run on the ModelBuilder toolbar.

16 Save the model and close the model window, then save the project.

17 One more time ... select a well then in the Catalog pane double click the model, then click Run.

Note that the model runs just like a geoprocessing tool in the Geoprocessing pane, but displays the message No Parameters - everything is preset from when you ran the individual tools before.

18 **Open File Explorer and navigate to and open the new Excel spreadsheet. After examining the results, close the spreadsheet.**

Rafael's question – *My Map pane shows the well feature I selected and all the selected properties like its supposed to, but I don't see the buffer polygon from this well. Where did it go?*
Not to worry – it isn't there by design! The only reason to make the buffer in this scenario is to use it for selecting the parcels. You don't really need to save it (unless for some reason you need to show it on a map). The output of the tool is automatically set to be Intermediate Data and will exist only in memory unless you change the setting. (right-click the output variable to see the options)

✔ Intermediate Data

Crea...

Unset As Intermediate Data (Ctrl+Shift+I)
Set the variable to preserve the output data.

Rena...

This is a pretty nice model in that it will repeat this process as many times as you want without error, but there is a limitation on its usefulness – it keeps producing the same output file. The model would be more flexible if it allowed you to provide a different name for each output file.

This can be done by setting one of the parameters of the Table to Excel tool function as a Model Parameter. Model Parameters are shown in the model dialog box when the model is run, just like a geoprocessing tool parameter, and allow for interaction with the user.

19 **Open the model for editing.**

20 **In the model canvas, right-click the PropertyList_Wells.xlsx variable and select Parameter. Note that it will put a little P next to the green oval showing that this is a parameter.**

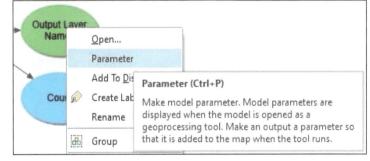

Remember before when you ran the model from the catalog pane and it had the message 'No Parameters'? Well that will now change and ask for the name of the output Excel spreadsheet.

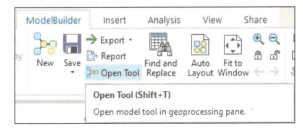

Word of caution ... once you set a Model Parameter, you can no longer run the model from the model canvas (physically you can but it won't prompt you for any input). From this point forward you should either run the model from the catalog pane, the geoprocessing pane, or run it using the Open Tool button on the ModelBuilder menu.

21 Close the ModelBuilder window.

22 Select a well in the map.

23 Move to the Geoprocessing pane. In the Search dialog type Well Property Selection.

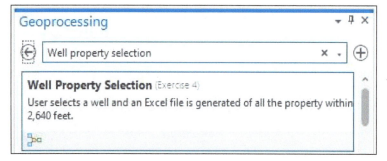

Can you believe it … your custom model came up as a geoprocessing tool? It even shows the tool description and if you pause over it you'll get the tooltip you wrote. Now you understand the importance of providing a good name and description for your models.

24 Open the tool and provide an output name of WellProperty2.xlsx. Then click Run.

25 If you are not continuing, save and close the project.

Rafael's Question – *When I run the tool and get the prompt for the name of an excel file, the words over the input box are the old file name I used in testing. How do I let other users know what to put there?* ModelBuilder doesn't really have a robust interface building system. But one way to mimic a good prompt is to make the variable name the actual words you would use for a prompt. To try this, edit the model, right click the output variable from the Table to Excel tool, and select Rename. Change the name to read 'Enter the name of the output Excel file:'. Save and close the model. When you run it the variable name will be used as the prompt.

This turned out to be a very successful tool and I'm sure it will get a lot of use. Things of note were that by running through the steps manually you checked the validity of your process, making sure that you had the right tools in the right order. Additionally when you got ready to build the model, dragging preconfigured tools from the History pane sped up the process greatly. Then adding a model parameter made the model more flexible for future use.

Rafael's Challenge – I would also like to have the size of the buffer be user definable. See if you can add that parameter from the Pairwise Buffer tool. This is known as **Exposing a tool parameter as a variable**. Hint:

The results should look like this:

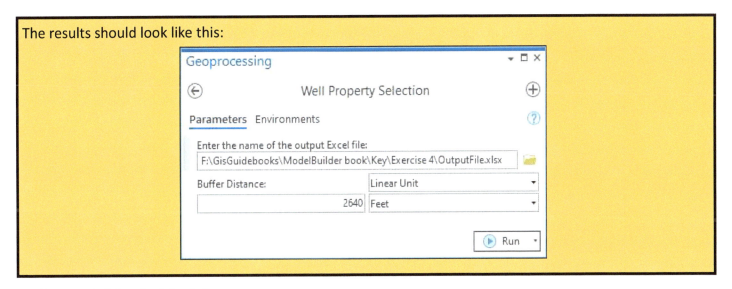

Using Variables in Models

Early on you learned that all the ovals in a model actually represent variables and can be used as parameters for model tools. The last exercise also showed that variables can be made user definable by setting them as Model Parameters. Once this is done, the user sets the value of the variable before the model is run.

Each of these examples of variables were derived from a geoprocessing tool, either as input, output, or a parameter of the tool. There is also a stand alone variable type in ModelBuilder that is not derived from a geoprocessing tool. These are added and defined independent of the tools, but can be used as parameters for tools by connecting them as you would any other variable.

When creating the variable, the user define the type of value the variable must contain. This can be a simple text or number value, but can also be something as specific as an existing geodatabase or an SQL statement. When stand alone variables are made into model parameters, the user must provide a value that fits the variable's type or the model will not be able to continue.

Stand alone variables can be created by clicking the Variable button in the Insert area of the ModelBuilder menu. They can also be created by right-clicking anywhere in an open area of the model canvas and selecting Create Variable from the context menu. This example shows the variable creation box and gives you an idea of the types of variables that can be created.

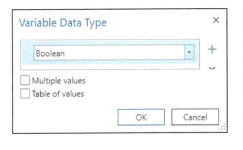

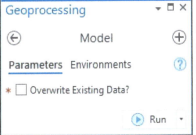

One of the most interesting data types is to use the Boolean type as a Yes/No question. It will be shown as a check box, and will return True when checked.

The exercise in this chapter will demonstrate the use of variables and the multitude of ways they can be used in models.

Exercise 5 – Configuring model variables

In this exercise you'll create and use a variety of different variable types. Then you will use those variables as parameters for various geoprocessing tools. For this scenario you will be compiling a dataset for Ellis County, Texas, that will include several feature classes containing data they will later want to analyze. Several of the feature classes already have a field to record in which county the data falls, and those layers have a definition query set to display only Ellis County. Other feature classes do not contain a county identifier field, so you will be adding and populating one.

1 **Start ArcGIS Pro and open the project file Exercise 5.**

In the Contents pane you will see the layers involved with this project. The ones that are turned off already have a definition query limiting their data to include only Ellis County. Once you add a new field to the other layers the County_Poly layer will be used to select the intersecting features so that the new field can be populated.

2 **In the Catalog pane, expand the Toolboxes folder and create a new model in the Exercise 5 toolbox.**

3 **Name the model ModifyCountyData and provide an appropriate label and description.**

Before you add any tools to the model, it's important to diagram out the process. It will follow these steps:
- *The user will provide the name of the new field.*
- *The user will provide the name for the County.*
- *The model will add a new field to the target layer using the user provided name.*
- *The model will use the Select by Location tool to select all the features that fall within the Ellis County boundary layer.*
- *The model will populate the new field in the layer with the value provided by the user.*

This process will be done for the City_Point, Tx_Gazateer, and TEA_SchoolDistricts layers.

4 **In the model canvas, right click and select Create Variable.**

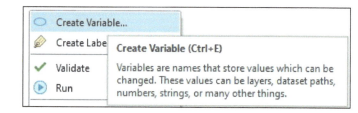

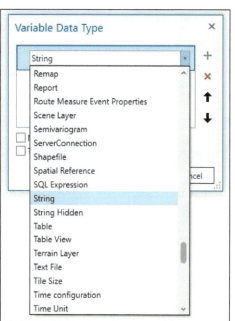

5 **Scroll down in the list and set the variable data type to String and click OK.**

6 **Right-click and rename the new variable New Field Name.**

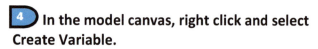

7 Add a second variable as a string and rename it Enter County Name.

8 Set both variables to be model parameters.

Remember that the variable name will be the prompt for the user. It's also a good idea to provide a default value for each variable you create. When you connect these to geoprocessing tools, if they are blank the tool cannot move to the Ready-To-Run state. This isn't critical but it will sure help if you have to debug a complex model.

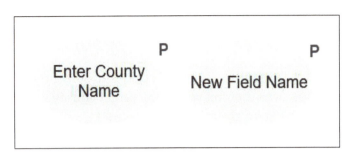

9 Double click the New Field name variable and provide a default value of County_Name.

10 Do the same for the Enter County name variable and provide a default value of Blank County.

Rafael's Question – *There's a TON of data types listed in the variable creation dialog, and I saw one called Field. Would I use that in this instance and how do I know what all these do?*
When you are creating a variable and setting the data type, it's helpful to think about what data or value this variable is intended to hold. Some variables, like Feature Class, will let the user navigate through the data catalog structure and select a feature class. Only valid feature class items will be displayed in the variable selection box so the user cannot choose an invalid item. Or if you want to know what geodatabase to use to store output files, set the data type to Workspace and only valid geodatabases can be selected. In this instance you want the user to type in a string that will be used as a field name. If you set the data type to Field the user would have to navigate to and select an existing field in a feature class or table. That's not what you're looking for here.

There's a data type called Any Value and one called Variant, but that's the coward's way out. The user can put any old junk in there and it may or may not meet the input requirements of the tool when it is used. Take the time to choose your data type wisely; it will be a big help to the user later.

As for learning what all these do, there's a list with the book materials called Variable Data Types.xlsx, These are derived from a list of Python data types and will be all the ones available to you. Some of the explanations make sense, others are used only in internal Python scripting, and others are very specific to certain databases or file type. Look through this list and you will get an idea of the variety of data types available.

With these two variables created and set as model parameters, you can start adding geoprocessing tasks. You will start with the steps to fix the City_Point data first, then duplicate that process for the other feature classes.

Refer back to the steps you outlined at the start of this exercise. The Add Field tool will be added first.

11 Add the Add Field geoprocessing tool to the model canvas (you should know all the ways to do this, select the one you like best).

12 Set the Input Table to City_Point.

13 Double click the Add Field tool to open the parameters window.

14 Under Field Name, click the down arrow in the input line. Note that the stand alone variables you created are present as valid selections. Select New Field Name and click OK.

The next step listed in our process is to select the city features that fall within the target county using the Select Layer By Location tool.

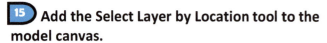

15 Add the Select Layer by Location tool to the model canvas.

16 Use the output of the Add Field tool as the Input Features and the County_Poly as the Selecting Features.

Finally you will use the Calculate Field tool to put a value into the new field, but only for the selected features.

17 Add the Calculate Field tool to the model.

18 Use the output of the Select Layer by Location tool called Layer With Selection as the Input Table for the Calculate Field tool.

To set the field name, you have to open the tool's parameters and set it manually. There's nothing in the model that will fit the required format if you drag it into the tool. However once you open the parameters you will see the new field name in the selection list.

19 Double click the Calculate field tool to open it's parameters.

20 Under Field Name, click the drop down menu and select County Name from the list.

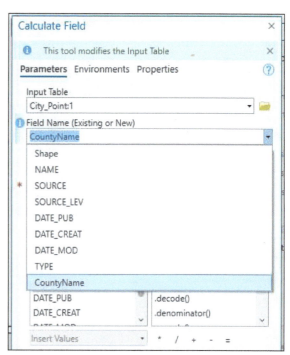

The next part is a little tricky. You have to use a model parameter variable as the expression on the field calculation. The expression will need to have quotes around it, but if you just put quotes around the variable name, it will use the name as the value. You want to identify the variable to use but have it read the value of the variable in the expression. You do this with variable substitution – which means that if you bracket the variable name with a % sign it will cue the model to replace the variable name with the variable value. Note that this cannot be done by dragging and dropping using the mouse.

21 In the Expression line under County Name = type *"%Enter County Name%"* (and yes, type the quotes and percents). Then click OK.

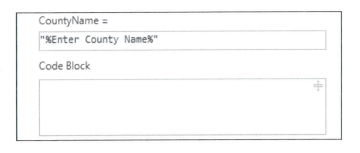

CountyName =

"%Enter County Name%"

Code Block

22 Save the model.

Your model should look something like this:

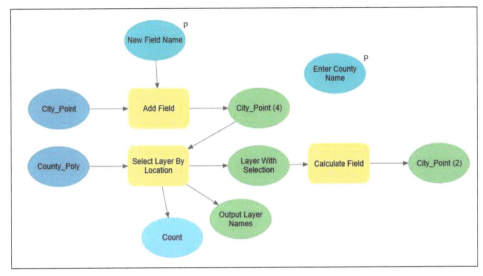

It wouldn't be a bad idea to test the model first and make it works before adding the code to process the other feature classes. Remember you have to open it with the Open Tool button, through the toolbox in the catalog pane, or in the geoprocessing pane because the model contains model parameters.

23 In the ModelBuilder menu in the Model section, click Open Tool.

24 Accept the defaults and click Run. If you experience any issues, go back through the steps and make sure you have configured everything correctly.

Since this model will be processing several datasets and could get fairly complex, it might be nice to use some of the grouping techniques from earlier to make the model look a little nicer. Start by grouping all of the tools used for processing the city data layer.

25 In the model, use the Select tool to select all of the elements except the two model variables you made and the City_Point data oval.

26 Right click on the selected features and select Group.

27 Rename the group Process the City Layers. Rearrange the elements to make the model more presentable.

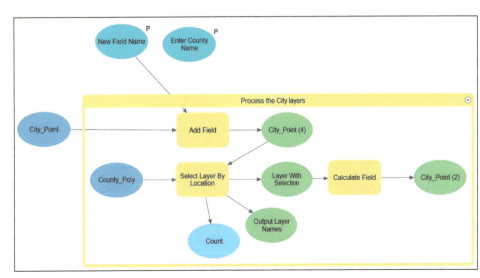

28 When you have modified your model to process all three target layers, save and run it.

29 Set definition queries on the three layers using the new field and new field value that the model created.

With all the processing done and the definition queries set accordingly, the data looks like it's ready for the county to work with.

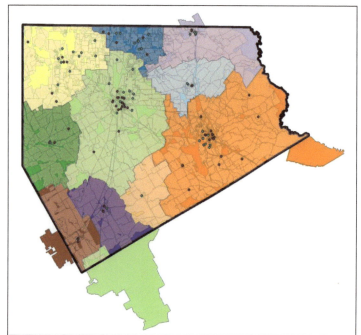

30 If you are not continuing, save and close the project then exit ArcGIS Pro.

That scenario involved using stand-alone variables and connecting them to geoprocessing tools much in the same way a model variable might be used. In this next part you will make some stand-alone variables but they won't be connected directly to a tool. Instead they will use variable substitution and link several variable together.

You saw the use of variable substitution in the Calculate Field dialog. The variable name, in that case, was bracketed with % signs signaling the model to replace the variable name with the variable value. These bracketed variable names can also be strung together as parameters in a geoprocessing tool, a technique called in-line variable substitution.

The process to create these is to either create a new stand-alone variable and name it, or use an existing variable from a geoprocessing tool and name it. Then the name is used in the substitution. In the example below, a stand-alone variable was created to accept a file name to be used in various tools. It has a default setting and the name was changed to 'New File Name'.

The buffer distance parameter from the pairwise buffer tool was exposed as a variable and given the name 'Buffer Distance'. Both are set as model parameters, and the variables names will appear as the prompt in the dialog box.

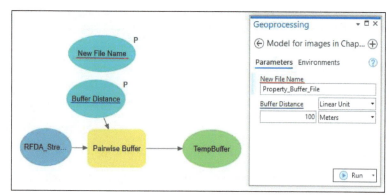

The variable names can then be used in variable substitution by enclosing them in % signs. Here the name of the output file is the New File Name variable, the Buffer Distance variable, and the added text '_Output'. The result, using the values above, would be 'Property_Buffer_File100_Output'.

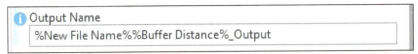

Output Name
%New File Name%%Buffer Distance%_Output

Rafael's Question – *Do I have to always include the percent signs?*
In the ArcGIS world it's hard to say you always have to do something, or you never have to do something because there can be many options. If you manually input the variable name for substitution and/or you are using two variables in the output then YES you have to use the percent signs. But some geoprocessing tools allow you to pick a model variable from a drop down list, and the subsequent entry won't display the percent signs. Just be aware of when you are using model variables and double check the formats.

Feature Class Name
New File Name
Model Variables
New File Name

Exercise 5a – In-line Variable Substitution

In this next scenario you will use more than one variable at the same time with in-line variable substitution.

You're setting up new project files for a large farming operation which will include a new geodatabase and new feature datasets. The model you create will prompt the user for a project name, a location name, and the project supervisor's name. Then the geodatabase name will be the project name and the feature dataset name will be the location name and the supervisor's name concatenated together.

1 **Start ArcGIS Pro and open Exercise 5 (if necessary).**

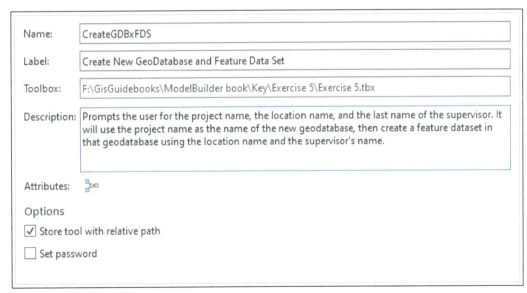

Name: CreateGDBxFDS

Label: Create New GeoDatabase and Feature Data Set

Toolbox: F:\GisGuidebooks\ModelBuilder book\Key\Exercise 5\Exercise 5.tbx

Description: Prompts the user for the project name, the location name, and the last name of the supervisor. It will use the project name as the name of the new geodatabase, then create a feature dataset in that geodatabase using the location name and the supervisor's name.

Attributes:

Options
☑ Store tool with relative path
☐ Set password

2 **Create a new model using the parameters shown here.**

3 **Add the Create File Geodatabase and Create Feature Dataset tools to the model.**

New Project Name: String ✕
New Project Name
Project_Name
OK

4 **Add a new stand-alone variable with the data type of String.**

5 **Name the variable New Project Name, provide a default value of Project_Name, and make it a model parameter.**

6 Create two more model variables for the location name and the supervisor's last name as shown here.

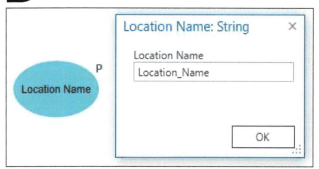

That completes the set up of variables. Next you'll use these variables as parameters for the tools you added earlier.

7 Open the parameter set-up dialog for the Create File Geodatabase tool (double click or right click and select Open).

8 Set the File Geodatabase Location to be the folder where your project is stored, and use the drop down box to set the File GDB Name to New Project Name.

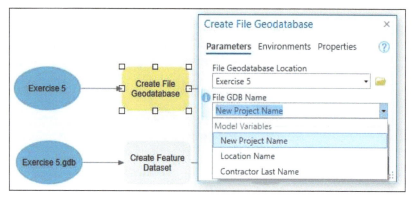

9 Connect the output from the Create File Geodatabase tool to the Create Feature Dataset tool as the Output Geodatabase.

10 Open the parameters for the Create Feature Dataset tool and set the Feature Dataset Name to %Contractor Last Name%_%Location Name%_files

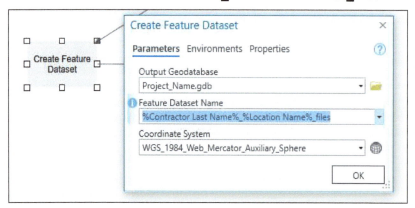

Note that the Create Feature Dataset tool had by default set the output location as the project's default geodatabase, and when you made the new connection the oval for that file was orphaned. It can be deleted if you like.

Rafael's question – *Do the spaces and underscores matter when doing in-line variable substitution?*
YES!! The spaces have to be included because they are part of the variable name. A feature dataset name cannot have spaces so normally you couldn't type them here, but because you enclose them between percent signs they are converted and the value for that variable is substituted.

The underscores are a good way to distinguish between the values in the feature dataset name, and are an acceptable character in the output name.

11 **Save the model.**

At this point the model should be ready to run.

12 **In the ModelBuilder menu click Open Tool.**

13 **Provide appropriate values for the inputs and click Run.**

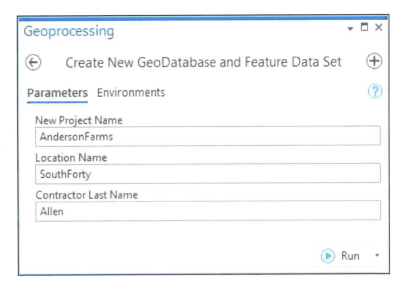

14 **In the Catalog pane, refresh Folders and view the results.**

Looking at the completed model, you may have noticed that the New Project Name variable has a line connecting it to the Create File Geodatabase tool. That's because you used the drop-down menu and selected it as a model variable. If you had instead typed in the name bracketed with percent signs the line would not have appeared. Notice that the other two variables don't have connecting lines for that reason.

15 **Save the model, then save and close the project.**

While not quite as robust as the input dialogs for real geoprocessing tools, using stand-alone variables with in-line variable substitution can give your model a nice look and feel for the user.

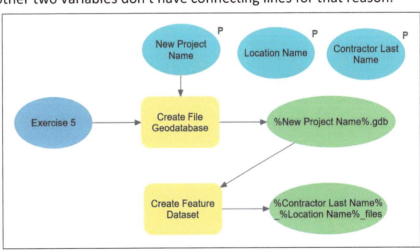

Model Parameters and Environments

There are a few background features of models that can give you more information about how a model works, as well as provide ways to set defaults for some of the parameters that your geoprocessing tools may request. In the ModelBuilder menu are buttons for Properties, Environments, and Report. You've seen how the Properties are set and the importance of having a good name, description, and tooltip. Environments can set a lot of the model defaults, like workspaces and default coordinate systems. And the Report can give you a detailed look at every element in your model, including how they are configured and connected.

In addition to these menu tools, there are tools within the model than can store valuable information, such as the metadata. Setting up proper metadata is the best way to document a model's function as well as a description of why it was written and it's overall purpose.

Exercise 6 – Setting Model Properties

If you've completed the exercises to this point, you've made some pretty complex models. Now it's time to look at the information about these models. The first to look at will be the Properties of a model. You've seen this before because it's where the name, label, and description for a model are set.

1 **Start ArcGIS Pro and open Exercise 6 from the provided book materials.**

2 **Expand the Exercise 6 toolbox and begin editing Model 1.**

3 **In the ModelBuilder menu, click Properties.**

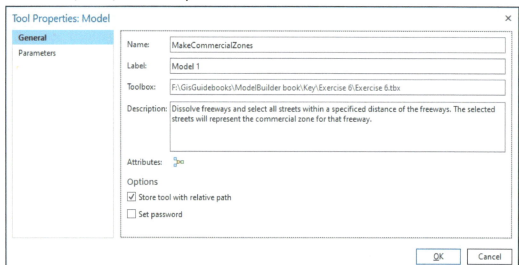

You'll recognize the first 4 entries. The two new things are at the bottom. The check box for 'Store tool with relative path' sets the model to use relative path names to reference the data locations for input and output. This means that if you pick up this project and put it in a new location, the model will still know where to get the things it needs. For instance, instead of storing the path for a file location as:
C:\GISGuidebooks\GIS Automation\ModelBuilder\Exercise 6 (the full path to the location)
it would store the location as
..\Exercise 6
The double periods means that it will start looking in the Exercise 6 folder regardless of what comes before it. This is helpful when moving projects from one location to another, or even if your files are on a removable disk that may be assigned a different drive letter on a different machine.

The next new thing is 'Set password'. It does just what you think – it sets a password for your model. Other users cannot view or edit your model without knowing the password, although anyone would be able to run the model from the Geoprocessing pane. And be careful about using this because there's no way to bypass the password if it is forgotten. (note - password was broken but is fixed in ArcGIS Pro 3.0)

4 **In the properties window, click Parameters.**

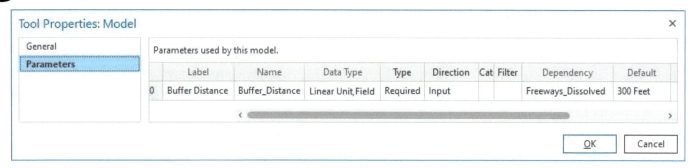

This model has a parameter that prompts the user to enter a buffer distance before it runs. In the Properties dialog it will show you much more information about the parameter including that fact that it is required user input. In other models, you may see this as output which may be files that the model is creating.

5 Click Cancel to close the properties, then on the ModelBuilder menu click Environments.

This massive list are all things you can set specific to this model. On a complex model you may have to set some of these values for each tool, and by setting them here the tools would automatically use the correct settings. In addition, some of these parameters can be accessed in your model using variable substitution. The settings available for this are the scratch workspace:

%scratchWorkspace%

the scratch folder:

%scratchFolder%

the scratch geodatabase:

%scratchGDB%

and the default workspace:

%workspace%.

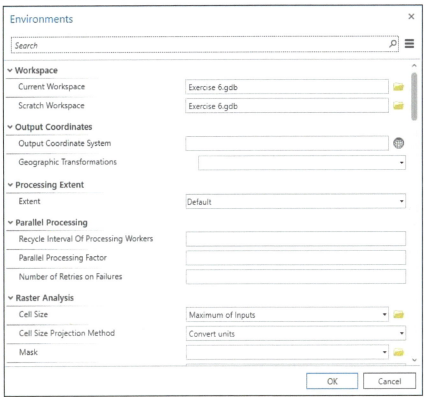

Rafael's Question – *Which of these should I set?*
You'll see that the workspaces are set by default, and you may have the case to set these to another location. After that, it will depend greatly on what your model does and what tools it uses or even if you are planning on using the inline variable substitution. As an example, setting all the raster analysis values would be pointless if your model didn't include any raster analysis tools, but setting all the scratch workspace locations might be worth it if your model uses these values in variable substitutions. So do this on an as-needed basis.

6 After examining the environment settings, click Cancel to close the dialog.

7 Next click Report on the ModelBuilder menu.

This will generate a report showing everything you need to know about all the variables, processes and tools in the model.

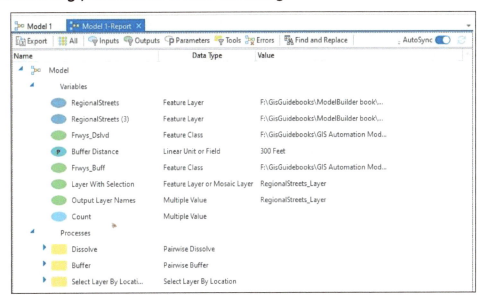

The default view shows all of the components of the model, and the menu across the top of the report allows you to filter the display to show only inputs, outputs, parameters, tools, or errors.

8 Try clicking one or two of the filters and note the effect it has on the report.

9 Click the Export button. Use the default destination and name, then click Save.

The result is an XML file that you can archive or give to others who may be sharing your models.
NOTE This file is supposed to open in a web browser like Edge or Chrome but currently does not. For this image I opened it in Excel **

10 Open Excel and open the new xml file.

As you can see, there is a TON of information about the model stored in this report.

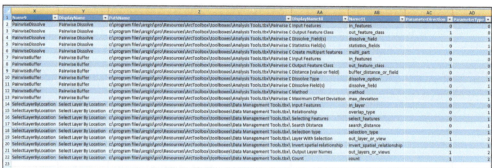

11 After reviewing the file, close Excel.

In the upper right corner of the report is a slider button AutoSync. This makes sure that any changes made in the model are automatically updated in the report. But it works in reverse, too. If you make changes in the report it will make the change in the model automatically.

12 In the report window move your cursor over the Count variable.

13 Click the Edit icon, then change the name to Count of Features and press Enter.

14 Now go back to the Model Canvas and note that the name of the variable in the diagram has changed.

The name or value of most items in the model can be changed through the report window.

15 Close the report and move to the Model Canvas.

You saw earlier how pausing the mouse over a tool will produce a pop-up that shows the tool's configuration. This can also be seen in the tool's pop-up configuration box which not only shows the configuration but also the environment variables and the property values.

16 Right click the Select Layer by Location tool and select Open (or double click the tool).

17 Examine the Parameters, Environments, and Properties tabs. When done, close the pop-up box.

Probably the most interesting setting in the pop-up box is under the Environments tab. Here you can set the output coordinate system for the tool. This can be helpful if you are working with data in a local projection but want the results of your model to be used in a web map. You can set the coordinate system to be Web Mercator which will make the output suitable for ArcGIS Online.

18 Save and close the model canvas for Model 1.

19 If you like you may on your own or as part of a class assignment open the other models in this project, noting their report and setup parameters.

At this point you should also look at the options for sharing a model with others. Models themselves cannot be shared, but the toolboxes that contain them can. A saved toolbox will contain all the models and scripts that you may have created and can be imported and opened by any other user. One note, however, is that when the model is used in another project, that project will need to have all the layers that the model uses. In most cases it would be better to create a Project Package which includes all of the data as well as the toolboxes (and subsequently the models) you have created.

20 In the Catalog pane, right click the Exercise 6.tbx toolbox and select Save As > 10.5/10.6 Toolbox. Use the default location, name the toolbox ExportedEx6, and click Save.

The reverse of this is for the other user to right click the Toolboxes folder and click Add Toolbox, then select the toolbox you sent them.

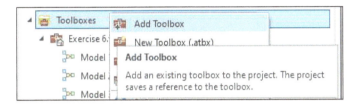

> **Rafael's Question** – *Why are the numbers for the toolbox versions greater than 10 when ArcGIS Pro is only in version 3?*
> Those numbers refer to ArcMap numbering. Starting with the next version, the toolboxes will show ArcGIS Pro numbers as well as the old ArcMap numbering.

21 Save and close the project.

Pay attention to the parameters and environments as you work with models. Sometimes the default values work but it's good to know how to set and control these when it becomes necessary.

Designing the Process Flow

Models are designed with a certain flow that should take your features, run them through a set of processes, and produce a result. When a model is executed it will first prompt the user for all of the model parameters that have been set. After that it will run in a linear fashion, following the lines of progression from one tool to another.

But the process isn't always linear. There may be some tools that need to run and complete before another tool can run, or there may be a condition under which one tool would run rather than another. One feature of models to help control this are precondition lines. These precondition lines can be drawn from a tool output to another tool, not to provide input but to say "don't run until this tool has finished". An example might be to have a process that redefines the coordinate system of a feature dataset, then a second process that publishes the contents of that feature dataset to a web map. The second process shouldn't run until the first process is done. Running out of order would be a problem for the web map.

In this example, the model creates a new file geodatabase and two feature datasets. Then it imports a feature class into one of the new feature datasets, but the precondition won't allow the Feature Class to Feature Class tool to run until the Create Feature Dataset completes. The Feature Class to Feature Class tool is using variable substitution to assign the output location to %New GDB%/%Web_Mercator% so if it runs prior to these variables being valid it will cause an error.

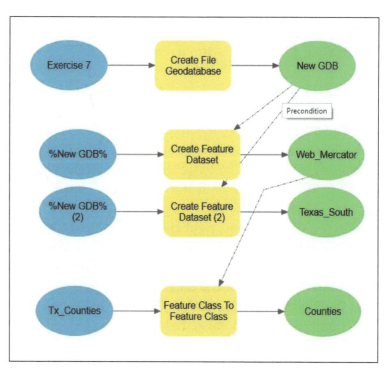

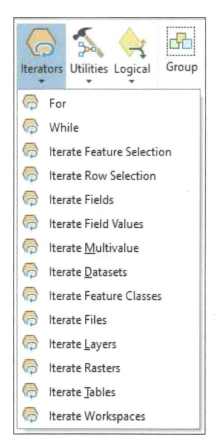

Another way to control the process path is with an iterator. These are model-only tools that cause a model to repeat over and over until the condition the iterator represents is met. Two of these iterators, the For and While, will iterator through the input data until a user defined condition is satisfied. These are probably the hardest to understand and use correctly, but with some practice you'll get the hang of them. The other iterators will repeat until they have processed all of the features in the input data and the differences can seem subtle. You can see in this list what types of iteration conditions can be used.

These can look confusing and some may look like they do the same thing, so it's important to learn what each does.

For – this is basically a number generator/counter. The user provides a starting number, an ending number, and an increment value. The tool does the math and runs as many times as it can within those parameters. For instance, you could say to start at 1, end at 10, and increment by one and the model will run ten times and stop. That doesn't sound very useful, but remember that the output of the tool can be used as parameters in other tools with inline substitution. Maybe you want to do multiple buffers around a features and the user specifies to start at 500, go to 3500, and increment by 500. Then you use the output number in each iteration as the buffer distance. The result would be 7 buffer rings, each 500 feet larger than the last. You might also include the buffer distance in the layer name with inline variable substitution.

While – this will run the model over and over until a specified condition is met. The user specifies a value. The model should be written to find a value and match it against the user input. The user then specifies if the model will continue either when the values match, or when the values don't match.

Iterate Feature Selection – The user makes a feature selection and the model iterates through the selected set. Features that are not selected are ignored. This will act upon a feature class or shapefile.

Iterate Row Selection – The user makes a selection of rows in a table and the model iterates through the selected rows. Rows that are not selected are ignored. This will act upon any table or database.

Iterate Fields – The user names a layer or table and the model iterates through all of the field names it contains. This is used to manipulate field values across the entire layer, not feature by feature.

Iterate Field Values – The user names a layer or table and the model iterates through each value of the specified field. This is used to manipulate the values in one field across the entire layer feature by feature

Iterate Multivalue – The user specifies a list of values, which could be layers, text, numbers, or basically anything you want. The model iterates once for each value in the list. As an example, the user may be prompted for multiple buffer distances, then a buffer and selection process could be done for value entered.

Iterate Datasets – The user specifies a folder, geodatabase, or feature dataset within a geodatabase and the model iterates through all of the data files it finds. This can also include a wildcard, a dataset type, and a recursive mode which would also process files in a sub-folder. As an example, if you point this at a geodatabase you could have it process all the Parcel Fabric files in all the feature datasets that have 'Prop_TX_' in the name. Or point it to a folder and have it process all the CAD files it finds.

Iterate Feature Classes - The user specifies a folder, geodatabase, or feature dataset within a geodatabase and the model iterates through all of the feature classes or shapefiles it finds. This can also include a wildcard, a feature class type (point, line, or poly), and a recursive mode which would also process files in a sub-folder. The major difference here is being able to specify a feature type. As an example, you could point this at a feature dataset and have it process all the polygon type feature classes.

Iterate Files – The user specifies a folder and the model iterates over all the files in that folder. A wildcard and file type can be specified as well as a recursive option. The file type is specified by providing an extension such as .txt or .xlsx. The output of this iterator is the filename with the extension and the filename without the extension. As an example, you could point this at a folder and process all the .XML files in it.

Iterate Layers – The user specifies a map from the Contents Pane and the model processes all of the layers in that map. It allows a wildcard and a layer type to further restrict what it will act upon. The recursive option here refers to layers within a group layer. Additionally the user can restrict by visibility or by validity, meaning that you could include or exclude layers with broken data links. As an example, the user could change the spatial reference for all the visible terrain layers in the Local_Elevations group layer.

Iterate Rasters – The user specifies a folder or geodatabase and the model will process all the raster type files it finds, again with wildcard and recursive options. In addition the user can specify a raster type. As an example, the user could point to a folder and import all the BMP files that start with ECHO_File.

Iterate Tables – The user specifies a folder or geodatabase and the model will process all the tables it finds, again with wildcard and recursive options. If the location specified is a table, it will only work on dBase (shapefile) tables or old timey coverage (Info) tables.

Iterate Workspaces – The user specifies a folder and the model iterates through all the other folders and/or geodatabases it finds, and it has a wildcard and recursive option. The user can also specify the type of workspace to include, with options such as file geodatabase, enterprise geodatabase, folder, or BIM location.

In addition to using an iterator in a model, there are two system variable substitutions that may be helpful. The first is a counter to tell you how many times the iterator has repeated the model. It's inserted as %n% and might be used to insert a version number in an output file name, or just to set a 'do not exceed' number on how many times your model runs. The other is a time variable that will insert the current system time using %t%. The format of the time is YYYYMMDDHHMMSS.

Rafael's Question – *I was playing with these and added an iterator to a model, but when I clicked the Iterator menu again it was all grayed out. What's wrong?*
You can only have one iterator per model. So after you added one it stopped you from adding another. However, you can have one iterating model call another iterating model. Perhaps you want to iterate through the layers in a map and do a selection, then iterate through the selected items. Model 1 would use the Iterate Layers tool and it would call Model 2 that would use the Iterate Feature Selection tool.

Exercise 7 - Iterate Files

This exercise will let you examine the different ways iterators may be used. It would take a lot of time to demonstrate all of the iterators but once you see some of the more complex ones used it will help you to understand how the others can be configured.

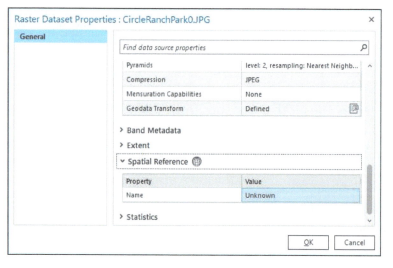

In this exercise you will use an iterator to process raster image files. The 12 files cover a new subdivision but they do not have a spatial reference (coordinate system) set.

If you added them to a project, they may or may not display in the correct place but you would surely get an error concerning the coordinate system, noting that it is unknown or missing.

The fix will be to define the spatial reference. It would also be a good idea to build raster pyramids and statistics for the data so that they will be ready for future analysis tasks. With 12 files to do, you certainly don't want to do these one by one.

All of the files are in a folder called Rasters in the project's folder, and they have the naming convention CircleRanchCreekXX.tif with each having a sequential number. You will use the Iterate Rasters tool, point it to the Rasters folder, and set a wildcard so that only the desired files are processed. The outline looks like this:

- *User selects a folder (model parameter for input workspace)*
- *Iterate Rasters tool – wildcard CircleRanch*, file type TIF*
- *Define Projection tool – set the projection to Texas State Plane – North Central*
- *Build Pyramids and Statistics tool – geoprocessing tool*

1 **Start ArcGIS Pro and open project Exercise 7.**

2 **Create a new model called ProcessRasters with an appropriate label and description.**

3 **From the ModelBuilder > Insert menu click the down arrow under Iterators and select the Iterate Rasters tool.**

4 **Search the Geoprocessing tools and add the Define Projection tool. Then find and add the Build Pyramids and Statistics tool.**

5 **Right click the iterator and select Create Variable > From Parameter > Workspace. When the variable is created, make it a model parameter.**

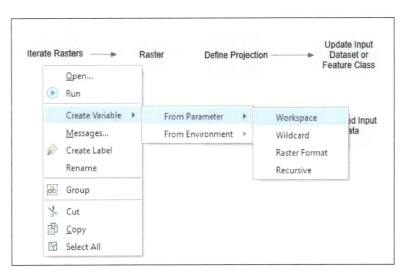

You can see that the Iterate Rasters tool has two outputs – Raster and Name. The Raster variable will contain the raster that the iterator finds, including it's location and extension. This can be used as input for other tools. The Name variable will contain the name of the raster without the path or extension. This is useful for making a list of the files that were processed or perhaps using it in an output file name where the path and extension aren't needed.

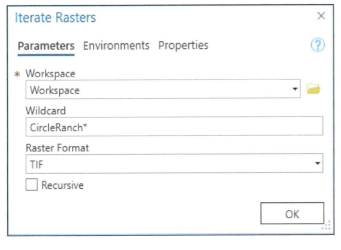

Next you will set the parameters for the iterator to have the wildcard and extension filters.

6 **Double click the iterator to open the setting box.**

7 **For the Wildcard, enter CircleRanch*.**

8 **Then use the dropdown menu to set the Raster Format to TIF, then click OK.**

Note that this iterator doesn't really need the wildcard or file type set because all of the files in this folder are to be processed, and they are all TIFs. But it's not a bad idea to set this anyway to keep the iterator from accidentally getting things it shouldn't. You could also set either or both of these parameters as model parameters so that the user can set them up when they use the model.

9 Connect the Raster variable to the Define Projection tool as the Input Dataset.

With the iterator configured, you can now set up the Define Projection tool. This will involve searching for the Texas State Plane North Central coordinate system in the dialog. It will help to know that the one you want is a projected coordinate system, in NAD 1983 US feet, FIPS number 4202. It's also the coordinate system of the current map.

10 Double click the Define Projection tool. The Input Dataset was defined by the connection you made in the model.

11 Set the Coordinate System to Nad_1983_StatePlane_Texas_North_Central_FIPS_4202 (same as current map) and click OK.

12 Next connect the output of the Define Projection tool to the Build Pyramids as the Input Data.

13 Save and close the model.

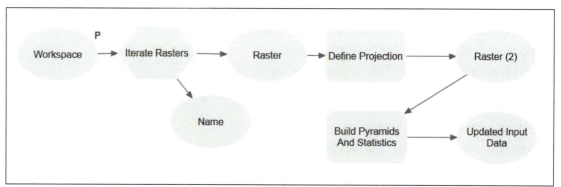

Rafael's Question – *My model is still grayed out … it won't run, will it?*
You are correct that the model doesn't appear in the Ready to Run state but because the first input is a model parameter, it will become Ready to Run as soon as the user selects a workspace. You could set a default workspace and make the model show colors, but it isn't necessary.

14 Go to the Exercise 7 toolbox and run the Process Rasters model.

15 When prompted, browse and select the Exercise 7/Rasters folder.

Remember that this is looking for a workspace or folder, not an individual file.

16 Click Run.

17 A check of the files in the Rasters folder will show that they now have a spatial reference set.

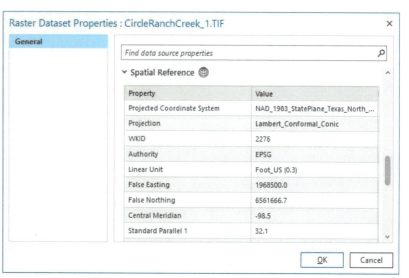

18 In the Contents pane, add a new Group Layer, rename to Circle Ranch, and add all the newly processed raster layers to it.

19 Right click the group layer and choose Zoom To Layer.

The images are in their correct location and draw quickly because of the presence of the pyramids.

20 If you are not continuing, save and close the project.

This type of iterator accepts a folder or workspace as input, then goes through the list of files it finds there. The iterators for datasets, files, tables, and workspaces work the same way – they go to a location and process the files found there. The differences will be in the file types you may set or the wildcards you may use.

More Iterators

Other types of iterators work with features in a dataset, including the iterators for Feature Selection, Field Values, and Row Selection. These types of iterators will go though a dataset feature-by-feature and perform some action against the feature. A feature class with 300 features will have the iterator going through it 300 times, however the iterators are quite fast at going through a set of features. It may even be something you leave to run unattended.

Exercise 8 – Iterating Through Features

In this scenario, the North Texas Association of Counties wants you to tell them how many antenna structures are in each county. You will build a model that can count the number of antennas in each county, then add the total to a field in the county dataset. The outline will be:

- *Add a Field tool – add a new field to the county dataset called AntennaCount*
- *Iterate Feature Selection tool – goes through each feature in the county data one-by-one*
- *Select Layer by Location tool – select the antennas that fall within the selected county*
- *Calculate Field tool – stores the count of antennas in the new field and the model repeats until all features are processed.*

1 Start ArcGIS Pro and open Exercise 8.

2 Create a new model called CountAntennas and give it an appropriate label and description.

3 Find the following tools and add them into the model canvas:

- *Add Field*
- *Iterate Feature Selection*
- *Select Layer by Location*
- *Calculate Field*

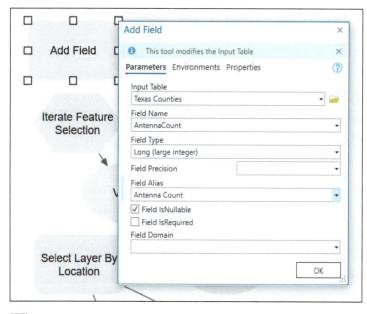

A few things to note about this model. First, several of the tools will not be used to feed data into other tools – they run stand-alone. You can use preconditions to make sure that things happen in the correct order. Also, the Select layer By Location tool produces a Count variable showing the number of selected features. This can be used in the Calculate Field tool to populate the AntennaCount field.

It is always best to configure the tools in the order in which they will run. This ensures that any requirements that a tool may need from its preceding tool will be set.

4 Double click the Add Field tool to configure it. Set the Input Table to Texas Counties, the Field Name to AntennaCount, and the Field Alias to Antenna Count. Click OK.

5 Double click the Iterate Feature Selection tool and set the In Features to be Texas Counties:1. Click OK to close the dialog.

6 Drag a line from the output of the Add Field tool to the iterator and set as a precondition.

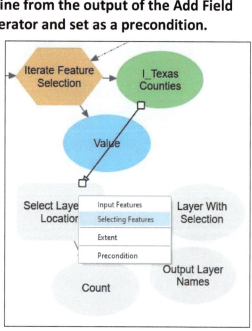

7 Drag a line from the I_Texas Counties to the Select Layer By Location tool and set as the Selecting Features.

8 Configure the Select Layer By Location tool to have the Antenna Structure Registrate as the Input Features.

The last tool to configure is the Calculate Field tool. This has to use the I_Texas Counties variable as the Input Table because it's the one that represents the currently selected feature. It will also need to use the field name from the Add Field tool, and the Expression will use the Count value.

All of this can be done with Variable Substitution, but first you will need to make the Field Name parameter of the Add Field tool a variable so that you can access the name.

9 Expose the Field Name parameter as a variable (Hint: Right click the Add Field tool and select Create Variable > From Parameter > Field Name).

10 Open the configuration window for the Calculate Field tool.

11 Set the Input Table to *%I_Texas Counties%*, the Field Name to *%Field Name%*, and the Expression to *%Count%*. Click OK.

> **Rafael's Question** – *Earlier you put a variable in a calculate expression and wrapped it in quote marks, but not this time ... WHY?*
> You have to remember what the field type is when using the variable substitution. The last time you saw this the value needed to be a string, so it was wrapped in quotes. This time it's a number and it doesn't require the quotes. Normally you could validate the expression to determine if you had it right, but in this case the substituted variables don't yet have a value and a verification can't be done.

12 Lastly, make a connection from the Count variable to the Calculate Field tool as a precondition. This ensures that the Calculate Field (which has to be run last) can't run until there is a value in the Count field.

13 Save and close the model.

That finishes the model set-up. Yours should look something like this   ----------------->

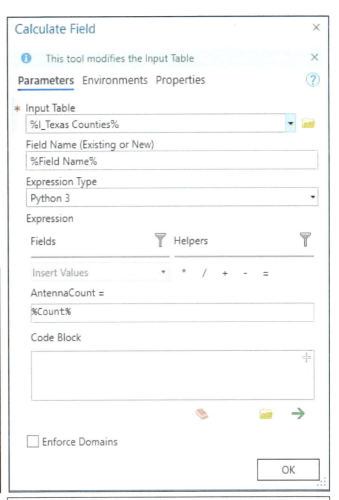

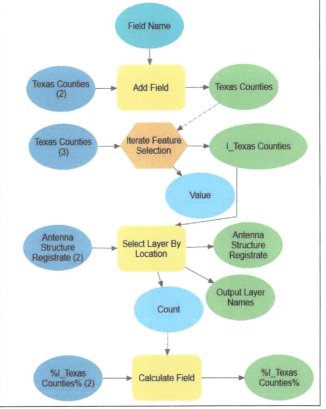

14 **Run the model. It doesn't have any parameters, so click Run in the dialog box.**

If you watch the map you'll see the selected antennas in each county flash as the model iterates through the steps.

15 **When the model finishes, open the attribute table for the Texas Counties layer. You will see the new field with the antenna counts shown.**

16 **If you are not continuing, save and close the project.**

The processes followed in this model are the exact same things you would do if you did this project manually, but by using automation the process takes only seconds to complete.

	COUNTY	Antenna Count
1	Tarrant County	210
2	Dallas County	123
3	Denton County	61
4	Parker County	61
5	Anderson County	53
6	Collin County	40
7	Shelby County	29
8	Wise County	28
9	Johnson County	25
10	Smith County	20
11	Hunt County	19
12	Ellis County	19
13	Cass County	17

Rafael's Challenge

This model does one thing using preset layers. It would be nice if you could use this to do summaries of any point features by county. Can you modify the model to allow the user to select a different point layer as the input, and also set the parameters for the new field that is created?
When you have modified the model, run it using the Texas Schools layer to get a count of schools in each county.

This model used the county dataset with 65 counties in it, but imagine if you had to process datasets with thousands of features. The effort it takes to design and construct a model will easily eclipse the effort it would take to process so many features manually. And the flexibility to use it on other datasets adds to the appeal of ModelBuilder.

Creating New Data with Iterators

The last exercise ran processes that altered existing data, but what about creating new data? You can certainly do this in a model that iterates, but you have to be careful when you create the output files. Merely providing an output file name might mean that the same file is written and overwritten each time the model iterates. You can control this by appending something unique to the output file name at each iteration.

One way to accomplish this would be to pull some value out of the dataset being iterated and append that to the output file name with in-line variable substitution. As an example, in a model that iterates through National Park boundaries to select and export linear trail systems in each park, you could append the name of the park to the output file name. It might look like this:

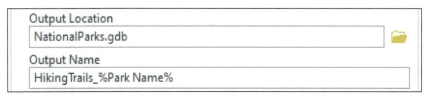

What if there wasn't a unique value that was suitable for an identifying file name, or if it wasn't necessary? You could also use the built-in system variable that counts the number of times a model iterates. Then the output might look this this (with the date/time value variable added):

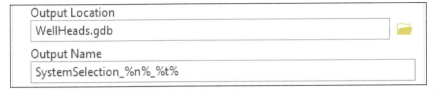

Exercise 9 – Creating New Files

In this next scenario you've been requested by the highway department to create a file for each county in the dataset with the roads clipped at the borders. This will allow each county's GIS analysts to do summaries and calculations for road maintenance requests limited to just areas within their jurisdiction. The process itself is rather simple but you will need to control the output file names. As a twist, they want this data in a new geodatabase with a new feature dataset.

If you noticed in the last exercise, the model did issue some warnings as it ran. With each iteration it was running the Add Field tool again and after the first time through it was providing a warning that the field already existed and therefore skipped the command. Because it was a warning and the tool knew how to handle this case, it didn't cause the model to stop. The Create File Geodatabase tool, however, will not be so forgiving. After the first iteration, the tool will probably halt the model when it finds that the geodatabase and feature dataset already exists.

The solution will be to have one model that creates the geodatabase and feature dataset, then a second model that does the iterations and creates the output files. The trick is to make a model parameter for each value that the first model needs to pass to the second. Here's the process:

Model 1
- *Create File Geodatabase tool - The user provides a name for a new geodatabase*
- *Create Feature Dataset tool – The user provides a name for a new feature dataset within the new geodatabase*
- *Stand Alone variable – Accept the user input for the data to be clipped*
- *Call Model 2*

Model 2
- *Iterate Feature Selection tool – Iterate through the county polygons*
- *Clip tool – Clip the streets using the selected county boundary*

1 **Start ArcGIS Pro and open Exercise 9.**

2 **Create a new model called ClipToCounties with an appropriate label and description.**

This will be the Model 1 described and outlined above.

3 **Add the tools from the outline for Model 1.**

4 **Add a stand-alone variable to accept the name of the features to be clipped, setting the data type to something appropriate. Rename the variable InputFeatures.**

5 Open the configuration dialog for the Create File Geodatabase tool. Set the location as the Exercise 9 folder, and use the line for the new name to write a prompt for the user. Click OK.

6 Expose the File GDB Name parameter as a variable and make it a model parameter.

7 Open the configuration dialog for the Create Feature Dataset tool.

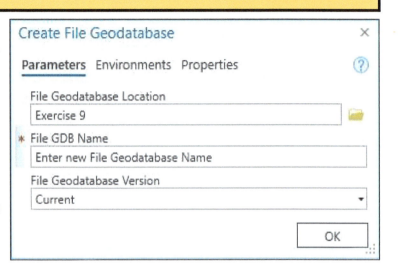

8 Use the newly created geodatabase as the output location and use the line for the new feature dataset name as a prompt for the user. Set the Coordinate System to use the same as the current map. Click OK.

9 Expose the Feature Dataset Name parameter as a variable and set it to be a model parameter.

10 Save and close the model.

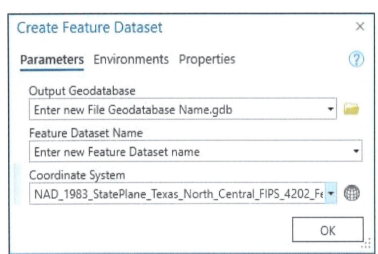

That wraps up the first model.

The user will supply three pieces of information, and this information will be passed to the second model.

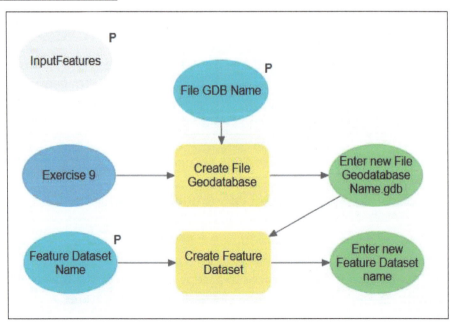

40

11 Create a second model called ClipToCounty2 and provide an appropriate label and description.

12 Add the tools described in the outline above.

13 Set the Tx-Counties layer as the In Features for the iterator.

14 Set the I_Tx_Counties output variable as the Clip Features in the Clip tool.

The model will always use the counties layer for the clipping, but the user has defined which dataset to clip and where to store the output files from each iteration. The output files will be the name of the new feature dataset and the name of the input dataset concatenated to the county name. The first two pieces of information can be learned from the first model, and the second can be learned from the counties file using the Get Field Value tool. You will add two stand-alone variables, each set as a model parameter, to capture the names of the feature dataset and input features. Then add the Get Field Value tool to find out the name of the county currently selected by the iterator.

The next series of steps doesn't include images of the dialog boxes, so pay attention to how you are setting the parameters. At this point you should be able to make the configurations without the additional help.

15 Make a stand-alone variable set as Feature Layer and rename it InputName. Set it as a model parameter.

16 Next make a second stand-alone variable set as Feature Dataset, rename it OutputLocation, and make it a model parameter.

> **Rafael's Question** – *Why do you need to specify a particular data type on these variables when it wasn't so important before?*
> In both these cases, the values will be used as a specific object in the second model so you have to make sure the variable type matches the expected input type. If you used String or Any type for the layer name, it wouldn't know that you specifically mean a layer in the map and wouldn't know that the iterator was selecting features from it. For the feature dataset, if this were a string it wouldn't be seen as a valid location to store files and when concatenated onto the other values would be meaningless. So you have to match the data types to the data inputs.

17 Add the Get Field Value tool and open the parameters window for the tool.

18 Set the Input table to I_Tx_Counties and the Field name to County.

19 Rename the output variable of the Get Field Value tool to CountyName.

20 Open the configuration window for the Clip tool.

21 Set the Input Features to %InputName%

22 Set the Output Features to:
%OutputLocation%\%InputName%_%CountyName%

23 Click OK.

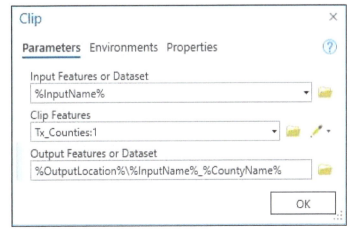

41

Be careful to get all the percent signs as well as the backslash and underscore in the output file name. The last thing will be to make sure that the tools run in the right order.

24 Make the County name variable a precondition of the Clip Tool. This prevents the clip tool from running until after the Get Field Value tool has been run.

25 Save and close the model.

This concludes the setup of the second model.

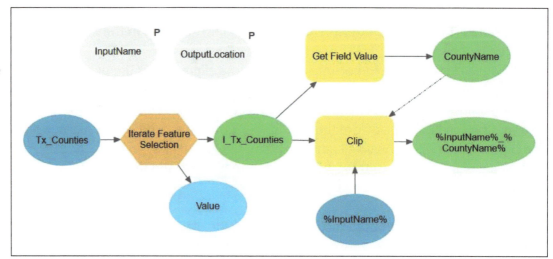

Next you'll go back to the first model and configure it to call the second model, making sure to match the user input to the second model's input parameters.

26 Edit the ClipToCounties model (you'll see it listed by the label you gave it).

27 Drag the ClipToCounty2 model into the model canvas. Note – it will also appear as a geoprocessing tool so you can find it from the search window.

28 Connect the InputFeatures variable to the ClipToCounties2 model and set it as the InputName.

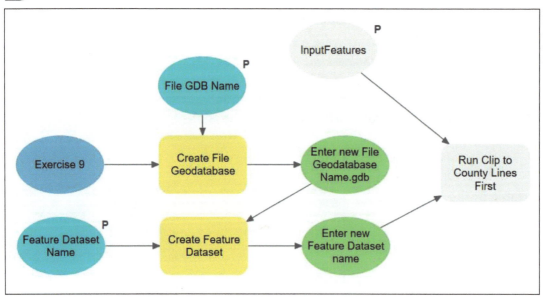

Notice how this is using the name you gave the variable before making it a model parameter.

29 Connect the output of the Create Feature Dataset tool to the ClipToCounties2 model and set it as OutputLocation.

30 Save and close the model.   Everything should be set.

31 In the catalog window, double click the ClipToCounties model to run it.

32 Set the InputFeatures to Tx_Highways.

33 Enter the name of the new geodatabase as CountyClips.

34 Enter the name of the new feature dataset as HighwayFiles.

35 Click Run.

This will take a moment to run while it clips and makes LOTS of new files. If you see errors in your model, go back and match the errors to the steps where the broken part of the model was configured and check that everything is entered correctly in the model.

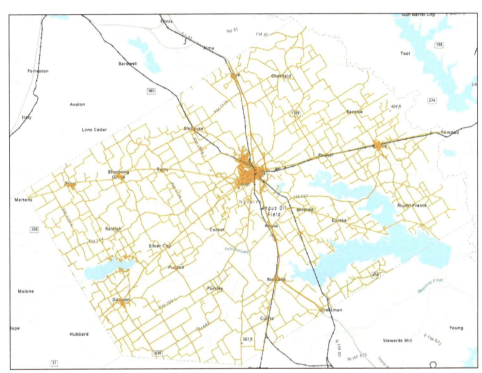

36 When the model finishes, expand the Folders folder and refresh the Exercise 9 folder. You should see the new geodatabase.

37 Expand the new geodatabase and feature dataset to see the new files. If you like, add a few to the map and check that they have clipped at the county lines correctly.

38 If you are not continuing, save and close the project.

There were a few tricks in this project that you may not have noticed. The first is that the feature dataset name that the user enters cannot contain spaces. There's not a way to verify that the user entered a name without a space so you're taking you chances that they'll do it right. You could add to the prompt to say New Feature Dataset Name (No Spaces) and see if that helps.

There's another that involves the county name. Since this is being pulled out as a value and used as a feature class name, you're taking a chance that the field value doesn't contain a space, which is invalid in a feature class name. In this exercise the data was cleaned up beforehand to ensure that the values were valid for feature class names, but you can't always be so lucky. In a later exercise you'll see how to add some error checking to the model and make sure the names are valid before continuing.

For and While Iterators

The iterators so far have been ones that go through a list of items one-by-one, which can be files, fields, workspaces, etc... But the action is pretty much the same. You name a thing, and the iterator process those things until it's touched every one.

The For and While iterators are a bit more complex in that you can establish a condition under which they run, and define when they will stop. So instead of processing all the items you point at, it will process items until it reaches a stopping point that you define.

The For iterator is fairly easy to understand. If you are familiar with the For loop construct in programming languages then you will see that this is very similar. You will define a low and high value, then an increment value that the iterator will use to check that it is still within the range of values you presented. When it reaches an increment value that is no longer within the specified range, the iterator will stop. For example if you give a low value of 100 and a high value of 500, then say to increment by 100 the iterator would repeat five times ... in the first run it starts at the low number provided (100) and it runs ... next it increments by 100 to 200 and sees that 200 is within the range specified and continues ... then it increments by 100 to 300 which is also within range and it continues ... and it increments by 100 to 400 and is still within range and continues ... then increments by 100 to 500 which is within the range so it continues ... and finally increments by 100 to 600 which is outside the range so it stops. Of course it took longer for you to read that than it will for the iterator to run through that range.

Setting the For parameters allows you to predetermine how many times the iterator will run. Also, the high range limit doesn't have to be an exact multiple of the iterator ... for instance you could set the range to be 20 to 40 and increment by 6. It would start at 20 and repeat for 26, 32, 38. The next increment would be 44 which is out of range, so it would stop after 4 iterations.

Exercise 10 - Building a For Iterator

In this scenario you work for the local water board and you need a way to count the number of wells within a given property for new permit applications. Not only that, you need to set up an incremental count depending on various other factors, so each search might not be the same. For instance an application for a shallow residential well may only require counts at 500, 800, and 1100 feet. But an application for a deeper commercial well may require counts at 1, 3, and 6 miles. Can you identify what the range and increment values would be for those two examples? Note that the values have to be whole numbers and your results will always be in regular intervals.

The model will require that a parcel from the Ellis County parcel layer be selected, then it will prompt the user for the low, high, and increment values. It will make a new table using the property ID in the name, then add a field called Wells_INCREMENTVALUE and store the count of wells that fall within the distance specified by the current iteration.

Try writing the outline of the model yourself first – can you do it in one model or will it take two?

It will of course take two models, but not for the reasons you might think. The first reason is because of the feature selection. In earlier models you were able to have the user do a feature selection on a layer, then feed that layer into a tool and the tool would only act upon the selected features. When a model has an iterator, though, it will ALWAYS act upon the layer as if there is no selected set and instead act upon all of the features. You can make a feature layer of the selected features in the first model which will contain only the selected feature, then pass that on to the second model.

The other reason for a second model is of course the creation of a new table. You only want to create a single table, so that needs to be isolated from the iterator. Otherwise it would make a new table for every iteration of the model. With those reasons in mind, the model outline will look like this:

Model 1 – Record Well Count
- *Get Field Value – extract the value of the PROP_ID field from the selected feature in the EllisCounty_Parcels layer into a variable called PropID*
- *Table to Table – make a new table called PropID_EXTRACTED VALUE that only contains the selected feature.*
- *Make Feature Layer – Make a feature layer from the selected feature(s) in the EllisCounty_Parcel layer*
- *Stand Alone Variables – three variables that are model parameters to get the from, to, and interval values for the iterator; data type is Long Integer*

Note – make sure to add preconditions so that the tools run in the right order

Model 2 – Record Well Counts 2
- *For Iterator – this will set up the iterator using the variable from the first model.*
- *Select Layer By Location – uses the feature layer from the first model to select wells within a distance specified by the iterator value*
- *Add Field – adds a field to the new table using the iterator value*
- *Calculate Field – stores the Count value from the Select Layer by Location tool into the new field*

Note – make sure it can take the name of the new table, the new feature layer, and the three For Iterator values as model parameters.

Rafael's Question – *Any hints before I start?*
Models will always throw you a curve because tools don't always work the same way when run in a model as they might when you run them from the geoprocessing pane. Add to that any bugs that may appear in the software. For instance, the Select Layer by Location tool won't let you use variable substitution for the distance value. It also won't let you set the distance units at all. But if you drag the For iterator's Value variable onto the tool's icon you can set it as the Distance value (even though it won't show up in the parameters dialog). Also, if you set the Output Coordinate System in that tool's Environment it will default the distance to the map units in the coordinate system. So just make sure the values you give are in current map units. For example, don't give values in 1, 2, and 3 expecting it to know these are miles if the map units are feet.

For very complex models, it's sometimes a good idea to make some dummy data and build a non-iterating model to perform all the processes once. Then go back and add the iterator and adjust for multiple runs.

These instructions will describe general steps and you will need to figure out all the configurations yourself.

1 **ArcGIS Pro and open Exercise 10.**

2 **Create a new model called Record Well Count, with an appropriate label and description.**

3 **Add three stand alone variable with a data type of Long. These will be the three For iterator parameters. Give them names to reflect what they will store since these will be the user prompts. Make all three model parameters.**

4 Add the Make Feature Layer tool using the EllisCounty_Parcels as the input and name the output file EllisCounty_Parcels_FeatLayer.

5 Add the Get Field Value tool with the input layer as EllisCounty_Parcels, the field name as PROP_ID, and rename the output variable PropID.

6 Add the Table to Table tool with the input as EllisCounty_Parcels, the output location as the default (Exercise 10.gdb), and the Output Name as Prop_%PropID%. In the Field list, remove all the fields except PROP_ID and SITUS_ADDR.

7 Make the PropID variable a precondition of the Table to Table tool.

8 Save the model, but leave the model canvas open.

If you've done it correctly, you model will look something like this:

-------------------->

9 Create a second model called Record Well Count 2 with an appropriate label and description.

10 Add the For Iterator. Expose all three values as variables and make them model parameters.

11 Add the Select Layer By Location tool. Set the Input Features to Well_Locations and change the Relationship to Within a distance.

12 Click the Environments tab and set the Output Coordinates to Current Map. Close the configuration box.

13 Expose the Select Layer By Location parameter Selecting Features as a variable and make it a model parameter.

14 Drag the Value variable from the For iterator onto the Select Layer By Location tool and set it as the Search Distance value.

15 Add the Add Field tool.

16 Expose the Input Table parameter as a variable and make it a model parameter.

17 Set the New Field name to Wells_%Value%.

18 Add the Calculate Field tool.

19 Set the Input table to Updated Input Table (the output of the Add Field tool).

20 Set the Field name to Wells_%Value%.

21 Set the expression to %Count% (remember that since this is a number it doesn't require quotes).

22 Lastly, make the Count variable a precondition of the Add Field tool.

23 Save and close the model.

That's a lot of steps to get through, and your second model should look something like this   ------------------->

Note the 5 model parameters along the left of the model. All of these values will need to be supplied by the calling model. Do you know which variables from the first model will be used to fulfill these?

24 Go back to the first model canvas.

25 Add the second model to the first model.

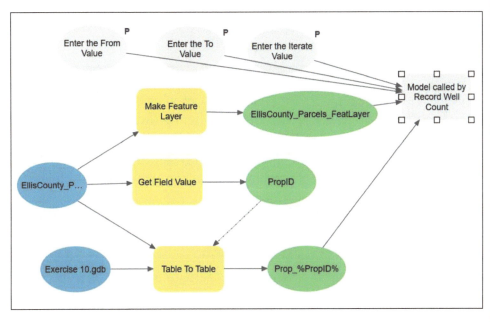

26 One-by-one, drag a line from the three For iterator values onto the new model tool and match them to their input values.

27 Drag a line from the EllisCounty_Parcels_FeatLayer variable onto the new model tool and set it as Selecting Features.

28 Drag a line from the Prop_%PropID% variable and set it as the input table.

29 Save and close the model.

Feeling confident? Remember that you need to have a feature selected before running the model, and you need to provide the iterator values in feet.

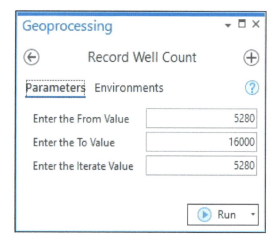

30 **Zoom in on the map a bit and select a parcel.**

31 **Run the Record Well Site model.**

32 **Set the From value to 5280, the To value to 16000, and the Iterate value to 5280.**

This will start at one mile and iterate one mile at a time until it finishes 3 iterations.

33 **Click Run.**
(if you get any errors, go back and read the error messages and try to determine where the model got off track)

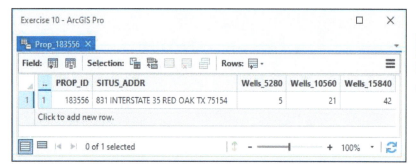

34 **In the Catalog pane, refresh the Exercise 10 geodatabase. Then find and open the new table.**

If everything worked correctly you should have a new table with the property ID, the Situs Address, and a field for each search distance populated by the count of wells within that distance. Try running with different parcels and different search distance parameters.

35 **If you are not continuing, save and close your project.**

Remember that the For iterator must be given integers as input, and the range between values will always be the same ... the interval number you provide.

Rafael's Challenge
The state has changed the application process and now requires a map of the location be submitted with the application. The map should include a visual depiction of the selection distances and show the buffer rings. Update the model to draw buffers around the subject tract at the given For iterator distances and add them to the map. For a bonus, use the buffers for the selections instead of the Within a Distance setting. Remember that when doing the buffers, you should add the %n% variable and maybe the property ID to the output name so that they will be unique.

The last type of iterator to look at is the While Iterator, and it can be one of the hardest to understand and configure. When set up the While iterator will evaluate a number to see if it is zero, or anything else. Zero equates to False, and any other number equates to True. The trick to setting these up is that the iterator itself can't do any calculations, the model has to do calculations and feed the result to the iterator for testing.

For example, you might want to select an air quality monitoring station, then iterate through the dataset until you have selected the next ten to twelve closest stations. The model would do a selection, then use the Get Count to to find out the number of selected features at each iteration. The result would then be subtracted from ten and stop when the condition equals zero – which means False. If any other number is returned, the iterator would continue since any non-zero number means True.

Rafael's Question – What if I'm looking for a count of ten and one iteration produces a count of 9 and the next produces a count of 11 – wouldn't the iterator run forever?
Sometimes you have to get tricky with the calculations. Suppose you divided the count by ten, truncated the value to remove all decimal places, and test for when it equals 1. Any value between 1.0 and 1.999 would stop the iterator. Just make sure your repeated selection increments by a small distance so that you don't select more than ten features in a single iteration.

Exercise 11- Building a While Iterator

The scenario for this exercise is that you want to edit your parcel database and be able to select all the parcels in a block. If you aren't familiar with parcel data, a block is the set of adjacent parcels bounded by streets. In this example each block is a different color and all the parcels that fall within a block will have the corresponding block number or letter.

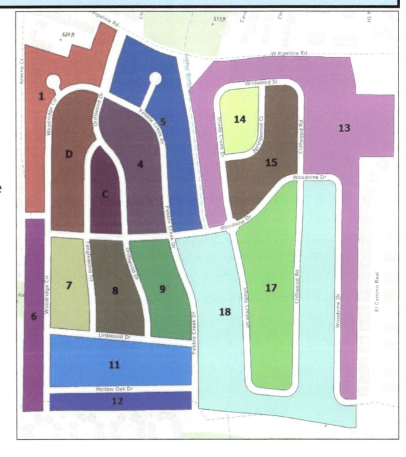

Someone has already started a model for this project but they don't know how to fix the iterator. You'll finish the model to accomplish the desired result. First you check out the existing model then complete the modifications.

1 Start ArcGIS Pro and open Exercise11.

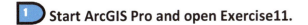

Input Features:
LandParcels

Relationship:
Within a distance

Selecting Features:
LandParcels

Search Distance:
5 Feet

Selection type:
Add to the current selection

2 Edit the model 'Select all parcels in a block' and examine the parameters for the Select Layer By Location tool (Hint: Hover the mouse over the tool).

You can see that it uses the selected feature in the LandParcels layer to select other features in the same layer that are within 5 feet and add them to the current selection.

3 Move to the map and select one of the parcels in block 6 (along the left side … doesn't matter which parcel).

4 In the catalog pane, run the model 'Select all parcels in a block' and watch the selections in the map.

You'll see that after running the model the parcels adjacent to the initial selection are added to the selected set.

5 Run the model repeatedly until the selection set no longer grows, and all the parcels in block 6 are selected.

The selections will no longer increase when all the parcels in the block are selected because it's only selecting within 5 feet of the selected parcels and can't jump the 50' street width.

The original author of this model was content running the model over and over until all the parcels were selected, then calculating the BlkNo field manually. It sure would be a lot easier and faster if the model did this automatically.

You will have to get the count of selected features, then compare that to the count of features that were previously selected. When you can subtract the two and get zero, it means that there were no additional selections from one iteration to the other, and all the parcels within that block have been selected. Then stop the iterator.

The trick that the other guy didn't figure out was how to preserve the previous count of features – and the answer is to get a count of features and make that a precondition of the next feature selection. Then get a new count and compare the two. For example, if the count of selected features is 7 and you do a Get Count, you'll have stored that value in a variable. Then if you set the selection such that it can't run until the Get Count is finished, you can get a new count and compare it to the initial count. The model generates new counts at each iteration. When the difference is zero, stop the iterator.

The outline, including getting the block number from the user and calculating the field, is this (try writing your own first and compare):

- *The user select a parcel in the map and notes the block number.*
- *Model Parameter – Prompt the user for the block number as a string*
- *Get Count – Get a count of selected features*
- *Select Layer By Location – use the selected land parcels to select land parcels within 5 feet and add to the current selection. (This tool automatically provides a count)*
- *Calculate Value – New count minus old count*
- *While Iterator – Stop if condition is False (number equals zero)*
- *Calculate Field – calculate the BlkNo field to be the user entered value*
- *Preconditions – make sure the Get Count runs first and the Calculate Value runs after the Select Layer By Location*

6 Create a string variable to prompt the user for a block designation and rename it 'Enter Block Number'.

7 Add the Get Count tool and have it get the count of selected features from the Land Parcels layer and place in a variable called OldCount.

8 Add and configure the Select Layer By Location tool to use Land Parcels to select Land Parcels within five feet and add to the current selection. Change the name of the Count variable to NewCount.

9 Set a precondition so that the selection won't take place until the OldCount value exists.

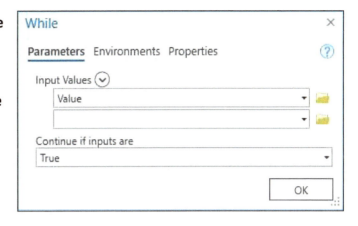

10 Add the Calculate Value tool with the expression %OldCount% - %NewCount% . Make sure the Calculate Value tool can't run until the NewCount variable is populated.

11 Add a While Iterator using the output of the calculate Value tool as the input value, and set it to continue as long as the result is True.

Rafael's Question – Do we continue if it's True? That sounds backwards.
Remember that a value of zero is False and everything else is True. When you subtract the old count and the new count, any value other than zero means that the number of selected features changed, so you haven't selected all the parcels in the block yet. So keep going … Continue.

12 Finally, add the Calculate Field tool with LandParcels as the input and the field BlkNo as the target. The Expression will be the name of your stand-alone variable. Note that since this time it's looking for a string, you have to use quotes as well as the percent signs.

Save and close the model. It should look something like this ------>

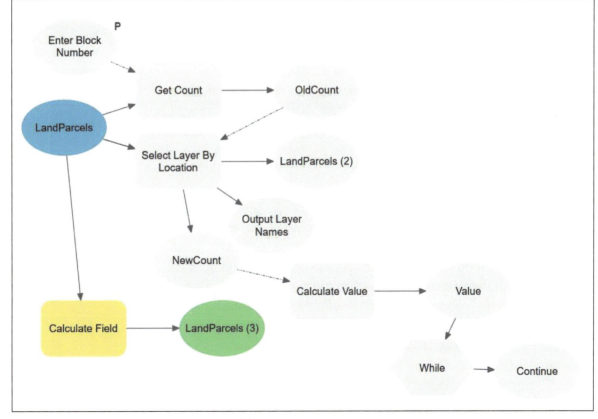

14 Select one of the parcels in block 6, then run the model.

15 Provide the block number as prompted, then click Run.

16 When the model finishes, refresh the map.

The updated parcels will turn green, and if you look the attribute table they will show the correct block designation.

17 Give it a challenging area and fix the block number for block 13.

Try more if you like, making sure to refresh the map after each run to see the results. Move to the bookmark Area 2 for more parcels to fix.

18 Save and close the project. If you are not continuing, close the project.

As you saw the While statement can successfully stop an iteration, but it's based on a numeric value being changed. You may have to get tricky to get the value you need for the iterator, but it can be very powerful if done correctly.

Process Branching

Yet another way to control the process flow in a model is with a ModelBuilder Logical tool. As you see in the list at the right these If tools can cause the model to branch to different paths depending on certain conditions being met (or not being met).

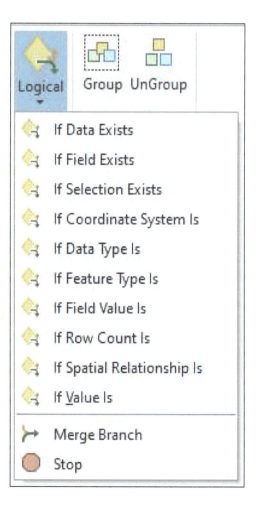

The output of each of these is either True or False. Then those outputs can be used as a precondition for any other process. If the output of the logic statement is True, then any processes using this as a precondition as well as any other processes downstream of it will run. Meanwhile, any processes using the False as a precondition as well as processes downstream of it will not be run. If the output is False, then the opposite happens.

The function of each of these If statements is pretty self explanatory – the tool will return either True or False in answer to the condition the tool represents … does data exist … does a field exist … is the value within a user defined condition … and more! Instead of trying to explain each of them and having the text get pretty repetitive, the following exercise will have you build examples using them with real data. The core of the model is already built and you will add and configure one of the logic tools.

Note that these tools don't cause a model to iterate, but they can be used with iterators. For example you may have a model iterate through a workspace and the logic statement causes the model to only process data of a certain type. It is possible to have more than one logic statement in a single model. Perhaps after checking the data type the model also checks to see if the spatial reference is set to a certain value. Just be careful of the preconditions used with these tools to make sure you are providing a flow that can actually happen. Linking the Build Raster Pyramids tool to the False condition of If Data Type is <Raster> would cause an error if the model tried to build pyramids on a polygon layer.

Exercise 12 - Logic Tools in Models

If Data Exists

This tool, like ALL of these logic tools, outputs a variable with the value of either True or False. It is up to you to decide how to use that information to continue or stop your model. These are sometimes categorized as If-Then-Else tools but a more accurate term is Binary Branching tools. There are only two possible outcomes, and you decide which (if any) of the outputs controls the flow.

This tool will check to see if a specified data element already exists. Note that it doesn't check to see if a data element has anything in it. For instance it can tell you if a feature class exists but not if it contains any features. The elements you can test for are Feature Dataset, Feature Class, Table, Data Views, Relationship Classes, Raster Datasets, Mosaic Datasets, Toolboxes, and Topologies.

For the exercise, you will go back to a model similar to one you made in Exercise 5a where you prompted the user for two names and used those to create a new geodatabase and a new feature dataset. What if the user enters a name for the geodatabase that already exists? You wouldn't want the model to crash, or worse to accidently try and overwrite any existing data. It would make sense to test for the existence of the geodatabase before starting. Also for this exercise you also want to make a new polygon feature class in the new feature dataset.

After using a logic tool, the model will be on two different linear paths since the logic tool will split the flow. To bring these back into a single path and allow more tools to be run, you'll use the Merge Branch tool. You very simply connect the ends of the two branches to this tool and whichever process finishes first will be passed along for more processing.

The outline is:

- *The user runs the model and enters thee values*
- *New Project Name - name of geodatabase / model parameter*
- *Location Name - part of output file name / model parameter*
- *Contractor Last Name - part of output file name / model parameter*
- *New Feature Class Name - model parameter*
- *If Data Exists tool - checks to see if geodatabase exists*
-     *TRUE - checks to see if feature dataset exists - stops the model*
-         *TRUE - stops the model*
-         *False - creates the new feature dataset*
-     *FALSE - Create the geodatabase and the feature dataset*
- *Merge Branch*
- *Create Feature Class tool - create polygon feature class with supplied name*

1 Continue with Exercise 12. Make sure the Demo Data 1 map is open and active.

2 From the toolbox in the Catalog pane start editing the *1. If Data Exists model.*

You will first add a check to see if there is already a geodatabase with the same name as the one the user entered. If it already exists, then you will skip the create step, and if not you will create it.

3 Delete the connection between the New Project Name variable and the Create File Geodatabase tool.

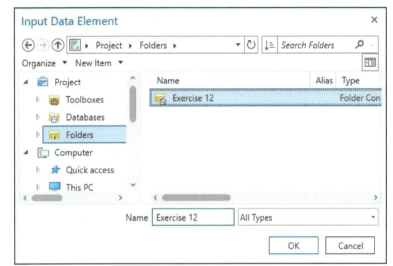

4 From the Insert area of the ModelBuilder menu, add the If Data Exists tool.

The Input Data Element for this tool will be the default folder for this project, followed by the user entered geodatabase name, followed by .GDB .

5 Double click the If Data Exists tool to open the configuration box. For the Input Data Element, browse to the Exercise 12 folder, select it and click OK.

6 Now click the value in the Input Data Elements line and add \%New Project Name%.gdb to the end of the folder path. Leave Data Type to Any and click OK.

By leaving the Data Type to Any, the tool will find anything with this name which is key because in the non-GIS file structure a geodatabase is really just a folder. You will see the difference when you add the check for the feature dataset.

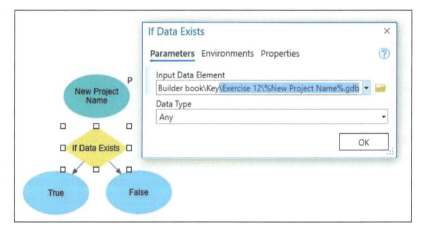

Rafael's Question - *Is there a way to test the model as I go to see if it's working?*
Yes. If you want to test this, pause your mouse over the True and False variables. Both should have a value of False (the default). Now right click the If Data Exists tool and select Run. Again, pause your mouse over the True and False variables - one changed to true to answer the question "Does this data exist". Now change the default value for the New Project Name variable to Exercise 12 and run the If tool again. Which output value is now true? Did this tell you if the provided geodatabase already exists?

You now need to set the model such that it will create the new geodatabase if it doesn't already exist. And if the geodatabase doesn't already exist then it's OK to create the feature dataset within it.

7 Draw a connecting line between False and the Create File Geodatabase tool and set it as a precondition. Open the configuration box and check that the inputs are still set correctly.

8 Right click and copy the Create Feature Dataset tool, then right click and select Paste.

9 Move the new tool up near the Create File Geodatabase tool and delete the connection to the original Create Feature Dataset tool.

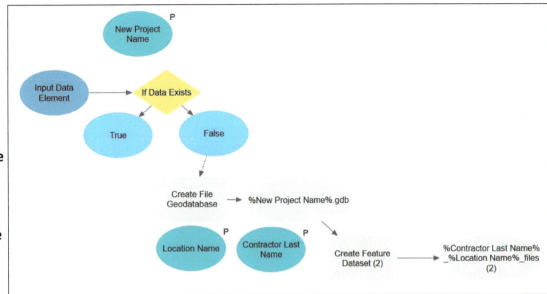

If the geodatabase already existed, you then want to see if the Feature Dataset exists within it. If it doesn't, then you will create it and if it does you will stop the model. Checking this is tricky because the path can get very long, especially in this case with the use of in-line variable substitution. The Input Data Element that you will check is the folder name, the geodatabase name, and the proposed feature dataset name. It will look something like this, with the <source path> being the location where you installed the book materials and data files:

<source path>\Exercise 12\%New Project Name%.gdb\%Contractor Last Name%_%Location Name%_files

10 Add a second If Data Exists tool. Open the configuration box and set the Input Data Element to the geodatabase name and feature dataset name as shown.

11 Change the Data Type to Feature Dataset. Click OK.

12 Connect the True output variable from the first If Data Exists logic tool to the second If Data Exists logic tool and set it as a precondition.

If the geodatabase does exist it will skip the create tool and go directly to the next If Data Exists logic tool. The second check is to test for the feature dataset. If it doesn't exist (False) then the model should create it.

13 Connect the False output variable of the second If Data Exists logic tool to the original Create Feature Dataset tool as a precondition.

14 Check the configuration of the Create Feature Dataset tool to make sure it is using the correct in-line variable substitution for the new geodatabase name and the new feature dataset name.

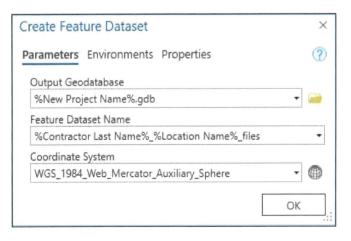

One more precondition to set. If the model has to create a new geodatabase, then you need to make sure that the Create Feature Dataset tool won't run until it exists.

15 **Connect the output of the Create File Geodatabse tool to the second If Dataset Exists logic tool as a precondition.**

Lastly, if the feature dataset does exist, you will want to stop the model.

16 **From the list of logic tools, add the Stop tool. Connect the True output variable from the second If Data Exists logic tool to the Stop tool as the input value.**

17 **Next add the Merge Branch tool from the logic tools menu.**

18 **Connect the output variables from the two Create Feature Dataset tools to the Merge Branch tool as In Values. Rename the output variable to New Feature Dataset.**

19 **Add the Create Feature Dataset tool and configure it to use the new feature dataset and the new feature class name.**

20 **Save and close the model.**

Your model should look something like this (with a little rearranging)

---------------------------->

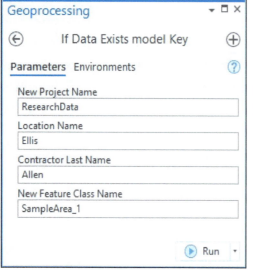

21 **From the Catalog pane, run the If Data Exists model. Enter the values shown here:**

<---

22 When the model completes, go back to the Catalog pane and refresh the Exercise 12 folder. Examine the new geodatabase.

23 Run the model again using different geodatabase names, different feature dataset names, the same geodatabase name, and the same feature dataset name. See if it behaves as expected, creating the elements if they don't exist and stopping if they do.

24 If you are not continuing, save and close the project.

You can see that the model got pretty complex, but if you follow the logic you can easily trace the flow of control.

There's a few things to note about this model that you'll see in more of the models that use the logic tools. First, the results window will display messages that a tool didn't run because the precondition was false. Those are tools that are downstream of the output variable preconditions of the logic tools. The model still has to look at those tools and determine that the precondition was false, and therefore not run it. These messages can be ignored.

Second, Rafael wanted to know why the Create Feature Dataset tool had to be run at two different locations in the model. Because if it only existed downstream of the True branch of the first logic tool then it would never run if the geodatabase didn't already exist. When the first logic tool would take the False branch it would never get to the feature dataset test.

There's a Merge Branch tool (explained later) that can bring two different processing paths together, however in this case you would be connecting the True and False variables to the Merge Branch tool. This doesn't work because Merge Branch accepts the branch the completes first, and both of these variables are updated when the logic tool runs. True would always win in this fight. Make a note in the upcoming examples with the Merge Branch tool that two geoprocessing tools are connected to Merge Branch, and whichever of those gets the True nod from the logic tool will run and the other won't.

If Field Exists

This tool will examine the field list from a shapefile, feature class, feature view, or table and decide if a specified field exists. In a previous exercise you used the Add Field tool and it would seem right that you could use the If Field Exists tool before trying to add a field. But in reality that tool has a built in check and will do nothing if it detects that the field already exists. The use case for the If Field Exists tool might be to check data before it's used in a geoprocessing task to make sure any needed data is present. For example if you are using Census data from the Living Atlas of the World and have many datasets to process, you might check for the existence of a particular count field in a dataset before adding it to the project.

The use of the tool is pretty simple. The input parameters are a dataset and a field name, with the output being True or False. But there's a twist. The user can specify a list of fields, seperated by semicolons, and the tool can test to see if any or all of the fields exist in the input table. It can also check to see if any or all of the fields DO NOT exist in the table, which basically reverses the True / False outputs.

For the exercise using the If Field Exists tool you will look at a series of parcel files, each with data from a specific subdivision. The goal is to get a list of land use types with a sum of acreage for each. A model has already been created to do the summary on one of the files, and you will need to modify the model to iterate through the files and do the summary. The catch is that not all of the files have the land use code field, called UseCode. If the iterator finds a file without this field it should skip it and continue on. The outline looks like this:

- *Iterate Feature Classes tool - iterate through the Dripping Springs feature dataset and process every feature class it finds*
- *If Field Exists tool - make sure the UseCode field exists in the file*
- *TRUE - Summary Statistics Tool to find sum of area by UseCode*
- *Use %n% as part of the output file names*
- *FALSE - Skip the file*

In the project folder is a geodatabase called HaysCounty, with feature datasets named Dripping Springs and Testing. Use the Testing feature dataset until you have the model working correctly, then modify it to use the Dripping Springs files before making the final run.

1 **Continue with the Exercise 12 project and the Demo Map 1 map.**

2 **Edit the model *2. If Field Exists*.**

This model is set up to do a summary statistic on a different dataset, which will be changed to accept the output of a Iterate Feature Classes iterator.

3 **Add a Iterate Feature Classes tool. Set the input Workspace or Feature Dataset to be the Testing feature dataset in the HaysCounty geodatabase. Set the Feature Type to Polygon.**

4 **Connect the output of the iterator to the Summary Statistics tool as the input table (delete the previous variable for this)**

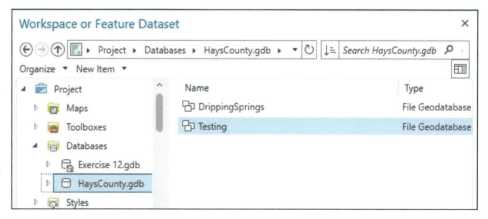

Next you will add a logic tool to see if the UseCode field exists in the current feature class. The output value of True will be used as a precondition for the Summary Statistics tool so that if the field doesn't exist, the summary tool won't run.

5 **Add the If Field Exists logic tool. Connect the output of the iterator as the Input Table.**

6 Open the configuration box for the logic tool and set the Field Test to "Must have at least one field" and the Fields value to UseCode. Click OK.

Note that you can have several fields in the logic test and specify if all the named fields must exist in the dataset or at least one of the listed fields must exist. Also, the drop down selection for Fields didn't contain any values - it populates this selection from the input table but because you are using an interator it doesn't know what table will be selected. Typing it in works fine.

7 Finally, connect the True output variable of the logic tool to the Summary Statistics tool as a precondition.

Even though the output of the iterator is directly connected to the statistics tool, it can't run if the precondition is not True.

8 Save and close the model.

9 Run the If Field Exists model and note the results (troubleshoot if necessary).

When you refresh the Hays County geodatabse in the catalog pane you will see a list of statistics tables, one for each input file. Each file contains a summary of area by land use type.

10 Edit the model and change the input for the iterator to the Dripping Springs feature dataset. Delete the summary tables generated by the Testing files and run the model again.

If you look closely at the geoprocessing results, you will see which files did not have the required field and the model skipped that step because the precondition wasn't met. These also didn't produce an output file.

If Selection Exists

This is the one Rafael has been waiting to get to because it is by far the most used logic statement. The tool's main function is to evaluate the number of selected features in a dataset against parameters you define. Note that the input layers for this tool have to come from the Catalog Pane in order to have selected features. If you point this at a feature class that's not in the map, it will never have selected features.

The online documentation for this tool is very misleading - you would think that this tool can only be used in a model after a selection tool has been run, but in reality it can test the count of selected features after any type of selection ... including a manual selection done by the user before the model is even run.
THIS IS WHERE THE REAL VALUE LIES!

Remember back in the early chapters when you built models that required the user to select a feature BEFORE running the model? And perhaps during testing you forgot and clicked run with no features selected and wound up with a mess? Or even had users do this and complain that their machines locked up trying to do all these selections? If you add this logic tool to the model you can check the selection status before the model even gets going.

Granted you can also use this logic tool after the model starts to check any selection done during the processing. For instance, you may ask the user for a value to use in a selection, but stop the model if the selection is null, or even if it's abnormally large. These kind of controls are very nice for keeping the model in check and keeping it from producing undesired results.

The input for this tool is any layer or view, then there are a host of conditional check you might perform:

Exists - has any number of selected features (even if it's zero)
No Selection - has no selected features
All Selected - all features are selected
Is Equal To - you determine the exact number of features selected
Is Between - the number of selected features falls within a range
Is Less Than - you determine the maximum number of selected features
Is Greater Than - you determine the minimum number of selected features
Is Not Equal To - you specify an exact number of features that must not be selected (any other number is OK)

Depending on the type of condition you selected, you can also provide the count to match against or the upper and lower ranges.

For the exercise you will modify a model similar to one you made in Exercise 2 to include a check to make sure at least one feature is selected when the model is run. Otherwise the model will stop. The outline looks like this:

- *User select a county boundary and runs the model*
- *Get Field Value tool - gets the name of the county from the Name field*
- *If Selection Exists tool - verifies that only one feature is selected*
- *TRUE - model continues*
- *FALSE - stops ... the number of selected features does not equal one*
- *Clip tool - clips the rail lines that go through the county and creates a new file called RailwayNAME.*

Note that the original tools in the model don't change at all.

> **Rafael's Question** - *Can I make a copy before I start in case I mess up?*
> Sure - just right click the model in the Toolbox list, then select Copy and Paste. It will make a copy of the model with an index number added to the end. If you mess things up or want to try a different approach, work from the copy - or a copy of the copy so that you always have the original model configuration.

1 Continue with Exercise 12 and open the Demo Map 2 map.

2 Edit the *If Selection Exists model.*

3 Add the If Selection Exists logic tool.

4 Connect the Texas Counties layer as the Layer Name.

5 Set the Selection Condition to 'Is Equal To' with the count being 1.

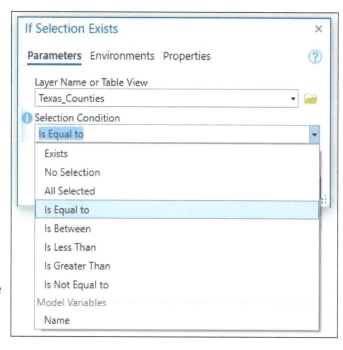

6 Make the True output variable a precondition of the Clip tool.

7 Save and close the model.

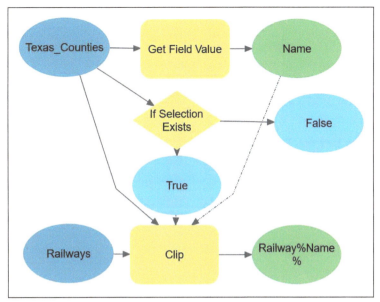

> **Rafael's Question** - *How did you get the connecting lines to bend?*
> Click the line to select it, then click ON the line and drag to create and position an new node.

8 Select a county polygon in the map and run the model. Examine the results in the Catalog Pane.

9 Try running the model with no features selected as well as with many features selected and see if the results are what you expect.

10 If you are not continuing, save and close the project.

The If Selection Exists logic tool can also be used to provide feedback within a model. Earlier Rafael asked about a way to limit how many times a model iterates based on the number of features that are selected. This logic tool does that, too. In each iteration you could get a count then test the number with the logic tool and set a condition for when it would stop the model.

The most important thing to remember is that this logic tool is testing the number of selected features and does not look at data values at all!

Checking Coordinate System, Data Type, and Feature Type

The next three logic tools on the list are pretty self-explanatory and you should be able to configure these without much assistance. Here's a guide to what they do:

If Coordinate System Is - decides if the input data element has the specified coordinate system.

If Data Type Is - decides if the input data element has the specified data type. The list of data types is the same as the list used to define a stand-alone variable.

If Feature Type Is - decides if the input data element has the specified feature type. Here is the list of feature types to check for:

Annotation	Line
Dimension	Point
Edge	Polygon
Junction	Multipatch

If Field Value Is

Now on to a more interesting logic tool. The If Field Value Is logic tool. This tool can work in two ways. For input it will accept a layer or view (with or without a selected set), then will test to see if a specified field has a specified value. For instance you may ask for a flood plane type with a stand-alone variable, then check to see if any of the features in your flood plane layer's ZONE_TYPE field contains that value. If you have a selected set, then it will check for the existence of that value within the selected set.

It also has the ability to check and see how many features there are with that value and allow additional controls. Similar to the If Selection Exists tool, it can match the number of features with the specified value against a high or low value, or within a range.

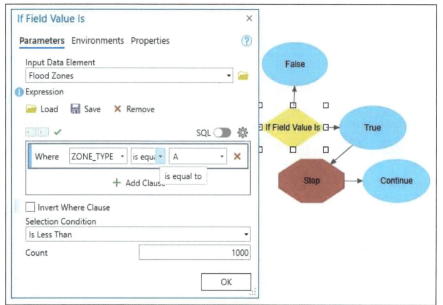

Using the flood plane example, you may want to stop the model if the number of Zone A polygons exceeds 1,000. Note that it has an SQL statement to find the features that match the value, then a Selection Condition to see if the number of features that meet the SQL statement exceeds 1,000.

Using the If Field Value Is tool is almost like having a Select layer by Attributes tool doing a selection, then feeding it into a If Selection Exists logic tool except that this doesn't actually make a selection, it just does it virtually. PLUS it can do this check on a previously selected set without changing it.

For the exercise you will look at the water well data again. The If Field Value model already has a step to take the user selected parcel and select all the wells within 5 miles, then it wants to export the file to an Excel spreadsheet.

You will first add a logic tool to make sure that only one parcel is selected when the model starts, then add a If Field Value Is logic tool to see if more than 10 of the WellType values are 'Spring'. If there are, then the model should stop. The outline is:

- *User select a parcel and runs the model*
- *If Selection Exists tool - make sure that only one parcel is selected*
- *TRUE - continue*
- *FALSE - Stop*
- *Select Layer by Location - select all wells within 5 miles (26,400 ft) of the parcel*
- *If Field Value Is tool - query for all features with WellType = 'Spring' and see if the count is > 10.*
- *TRUE - Stop*
- *FALSE - continue*
- *Table to Excel - export the table to an Excel file prompting the user for the name of the output file*

1 Continue with Exercise 12 and open Demo Map 3.

2 Edit the If Field Value Is model.

3 Add a If Selection Exists tool and configure it to continue only if a single parcel is selected.

4 Add a If Field Value Is tool.

5 Set the Input Data Element to the output of the Select Layer by Location tool.

6 Use the query builder to make the statement WellType is equal to Spring.

7 Change the Selection Condition to Is Greater Than and the Count to 10. Click OK.

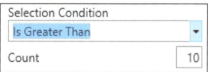

8 Connect the False output variable of the If Field Value Is logic tool to the Table to Excel tool as a precondition.

9 Save and close the model.

That should do it:
------------------------->

10 Run the model first with no parcels selected; then with one selected, then with more than one selected. Did it perform as expected?

11 Open the Excel file that was created and examine the results. Close when finished.

12 If not continuing, save and close the project.

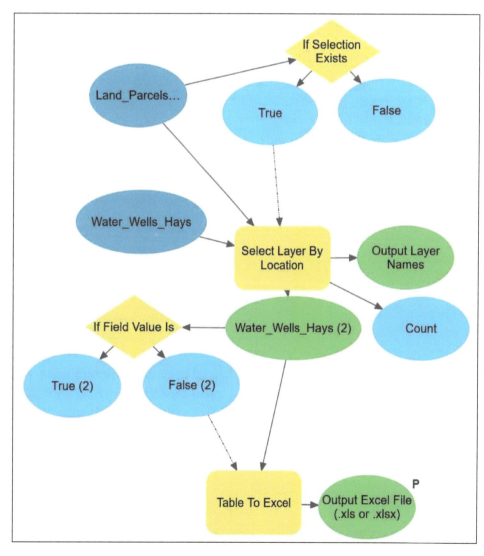

Note that the logic tool didn't affect the number of wells that are selected and ultimately exported to the Excel file. The file contains wells of all types even though you scrutinized the count of Spring wells to control the process.

If Row Count Is

Next on the hit parade of logic tools is the If Row Count Is logic tool. This tool functions exactly the same as the If Selection Exists logic tool except that the If Row Count Is logic tool does not test for the cases of All records selected or No records selected. Given the choice, use the If Selection Exists logic tool.

On to the If Spatial Relationship Is logic tool. This one is really fascinating and does something that no other model tool can ... it can test spatial relationships on the fly. For example, after a selection set is made it can test the selection to see if it intersects another dataset and report back how many features meet the spatial relationship. Then like the other logic tools that do a virtual manipulation of the data you can have the model make decisions based on the reported feature count - again with greater than/less than, between, equal/not equal to, and all/no features selected. It's the equivalent of combining a Select Layer by Location tool and the If Selection Exists logic tool into a virtual process.

For the exercise you will work with the Texas schools data again, matching it to the county datasets. The State Comptroller wants a list of all schools that are in a county with ten or more school districts. See if you can come up with a plan of attack before looking at the outline here:

- *Iterate Feature Selection tool - iterate through the county features*
- *If Spatial Relationship Is logic tool - test to see if the selected county intersects more than 9 school districts*
- *Get Field Value - get the value of the field CountyName to use in output file name*
- *TRUE - Select Layer By Location tool - select schools that intersect selected county*
- *Table to Excel - output selected rows to an excel spreadsheet called TEA_Schools_COUNTYNAME*
- *FALSE - iterate to next polygon*

Build this using the layers in the Test Data group, then once things are working change to use the data in the School Data group.

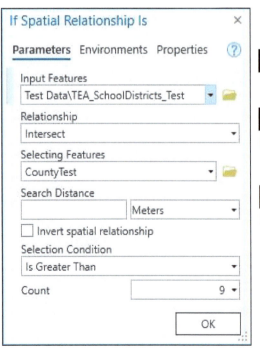

1️⃣ **Continue with Exercise 12 and move to the Demo Map 4 map.**

2️⃣ **Look at these two images and build this model. (you should know how by now!)**

3️⃣ **Test it using the Test Data, then run again with the full set of School Data.**

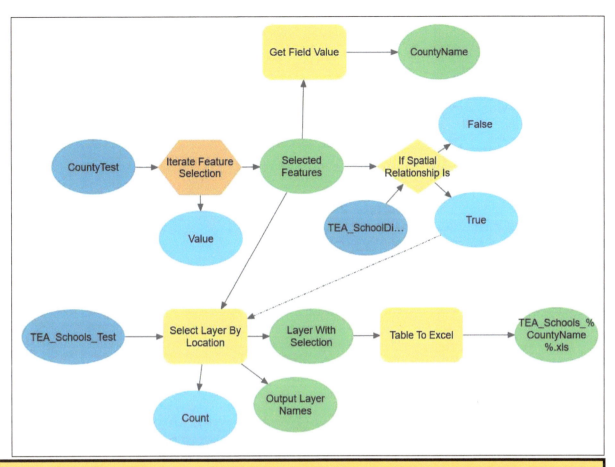

If Value Is

The last IF logic tool in the list is the If Value Is logic tool, which will accept any input value and match it against a value or list of values to see if it matches. Remember that the If Field Value Is logic tool can only check values that are already in an attribute table, but this one can accept user input, output from another tool, or even a value calculated on-the-fly in the model.

The input is compared to the test values using one of these conditions:

Is equal to at least one value	Is less than
Does not match at least one value	Is greater than
Does not match every value	Is less than or equal to
Is between any one range of values	Is greater than or equal to
Is not between any range of values	Is empty

For the exercise you will also use a new tool called Calculate Value tool. This tool acts as a vessel for running Python code within a model. The code may be a simple one-line expression or a block of code that can take values from the model and perform complex calculations. The first model you build for this exercise will use a simple expression but the next will use more code.

The scenario is that you are presented with a set of parcel data that includes the appraised value from 2012 and 2022. The City Manager wants to see a map and an excel spreadsheet with a column showing a change category.

The categories show that the percent change in value is a Minor Increase (0% to 20%), a Significant Increase (20.01% to 45%), a Major Increase (45.01% to 60%), or is Over 60% (Greater Than 60%). You will iterate through the parcels and do the calculation and assignment of the correct category one-by-one. The Calculate Value tool can be used to calculate the percent change in appraised value, then the If Value Is tool can be used to decide what range the value falls in, and the Calculate Field tool can be used to populate the Change Description field.

The formula for calculating the percent change in difference between two values is:
*((New Value - Old Value) / Old Value) * 100*

The outline looks like this:

- *Run the Model*
- *Iterate Feature Selection tool - set the In Features to be Land Records.*
- *Get Field Value tool - get the value of the Value 2021 field as Long integer and rename Val21*
- *Get Field Value tool - get the value of the Val2022 field as Long integer and rename Val22*
- *Calculate Value tool - ((%Val22% - %Val21%)/%Val21%)*100 and rename PcntChange*
- *If Value Is tool - Compare the PcntChange value to be less than 20*
- *TRUE - Calculate Field Tool - set Change Description field to Minor Increase*
- *FALSE - Next If Value Is tool ...*
- *(2) If Value Is tool - compare PcntChange value to be bewtween 20.00001 and 45*
- *TRUE - Calculate Field Tool - set Change Description field to Significant Increase*
- *FALSE - Next If Value Is tool ...*
- *(3) If Value Is tool - Compare the PcntChange value to be between 25.00001 and 60*
- *TRUE - Calculate Field Tool - set Change Description field to Major Increase*
- *FALSE - Calculate Field Tool - set Change Description field to Greater Than 60% Increase*
- *Model repeats with the Iterator*

There is a Land Records - Test dataset with fewer features that you should use until the model running correctly. The model doesn't process features very quickly; about 100 records a minute. So the test dataset will take about 5 minutes to complete and the full dataset might take as much as 15 minutes to complete.

Instead of full step-by-step instructions on this one, you should be able to build this model with just a few hints.

* Use Demo Map 5 and the existing If Value Is model.

* You've set up iterators before, and used the Get Field Value tool before, so no help should be needed there.

* Take the time to rename all of your output variables so that you can more easily follow their use in the model.

* The Calculate Value tool has an Expression line for the calculation you want to do, and a Code Block below for more complex calculations. For this model you only need to put the formula shown here in the Expression line. ------------------------->

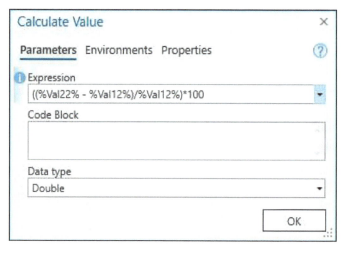

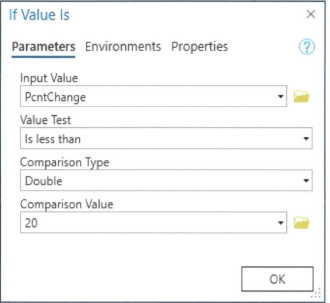

* The first If Value Is logic tool is set to be Less Than with a Comparison Value of 20.

<------------------------------

* The first (and all) Calculate Field tools are set to put a text value in the Change Description field depending on which value you tested for.

* The second and third If Value Is logic tools use the 'Is between any one range of values' setting for the Value Test. Then you put in the low and high values for the range.

----------------------------------->

* After the last value check you can use the False output to go to the last Calculate Field tool since at this point the test value has to be higher than the previous comparison values.
* This is a hard model - take your time and follow the flow of values.

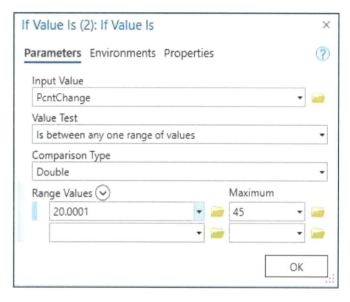

The finished model will look something like this:

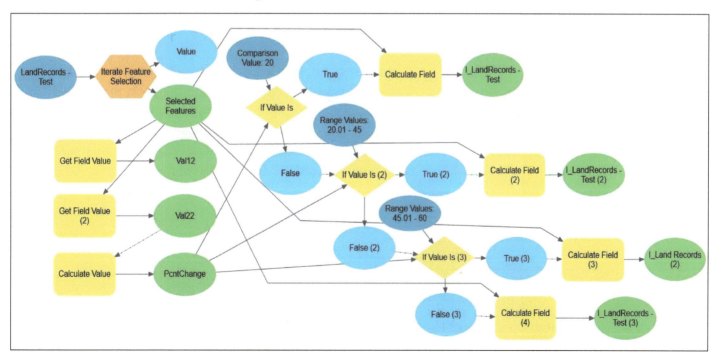

When you run the model with the model canvas open, you can see it making the decisions and flowing the values to the correct tools.

That wraps up the logic tools! These are the most powerful things you can add to any model because of their ability to make decisions and branch the model into different paths.   ……. except maybe for Python ….

Python in a Model

You saw in the exercises for the logic tools that the Calculate Value tool is designed as a vessel for Python code to be run within a model. And of course the more Python you know, and the ArcGIS Python module ArcPy, the more powerful you can make this tool.

The top line of the tool is the Expression line and can be either a simple formula (like you used in Exercise 12) or code that defines a function and calls Python code in the Code Block window. The expression formula can include any variable substitutions and Python functions. For example, you could round a number to one decimal place with the Python function Round() like this ------------------>

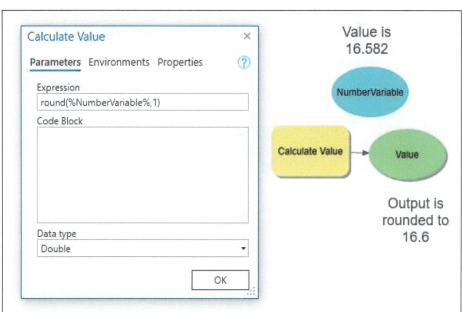

Any of the simple Python functions can be used provided that you can complete them on a single line.

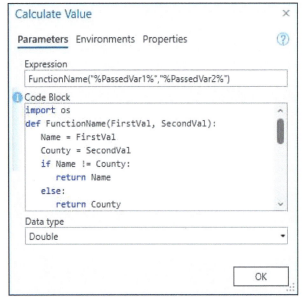

For a more complex Python code, you use the Expression line to call a function and pass values to the Code Block. Then the Code Block defines a programming function and reads in the passed values. After this the code can pretty much do anything you want with Python and ArcPy and use the return command to send values back to the model.

This book will only demonstrate a simple Python If-Then-Else example. To learn more about Python and the ArcPy module you can get the book GIS Tutorial for Python Scripting at the GISGuidebooks.com website. It's an ArcMap book with hands-on exercises like this book, and the lessons will apply to ArcGIS Pro as well.

Exercise 13 – Programming the Calculate Value tool

In this scenario you will revisit the model you wrote in Exercise 12 for the If Value Is logic tool. It went through a long and tedious branching process to determine the percent change in value, and hence the value for the Change Description field. *But it w a s   s o o o   s l o o o w w w.* At about one record per second it was all you could do to have it process a few hundred records. Image if you had to do that for an entire county-wide dataset? The Python processing should go a lot quicker and make for a simpler model, so you will re-write that model using a Calculate Value tool with some Python code. The outline should look like this:

- *Iterate Feature Selection logic tool – iterate through the dataset*
- *Get Field Value tool – extract the value from the Value 2012 field*
- *Get Field Value tool – extract the value from the Value 2022 field*
- *Calculate Value tool – perform the percent change calculation, then use an If-Then-Else process to return the correct Change Description using Python code within the tool*
- *Calculate Field tool – use the output of the Calculate Value tool and define the value of the Change Description field*

As with the last exercise, you should know how to configure all of the tools with the exception of putting the Python code in the Calculate Value tool. This part will be explained step-by-step.

1 **Open Exercise 13.**

The model Process Parcels for Percent Change already exists with all the tools in place, just like they were in Exercise 12. What's missing is the code for the Calculate Value tool, which you will need to add.

If you are familiar with using a Python code editor, you know that a lot of the indentations and code formatting is done automatically. This speeds up code writing and in many cases prevents spacing and formatting errors. This code window has none of that! To indent you will use spaces (not tabs), and for a second level of indents you will add more spaces. It's important that your indents be equal for the sections of code, so a good practice is to use three spaces for the first indents, three more for the next, and so on. Use the return command to determine what value the Calculate Value tool will send back to the model. This command will appear within each branch of the if statement. And Python is case sensitive, so be careful!

2 **Open the configuration window for the Calculate Value tool. Enter the code shown here** ------------------------->

This code can be found in a file called Ex13Code.txt in the book materials download.

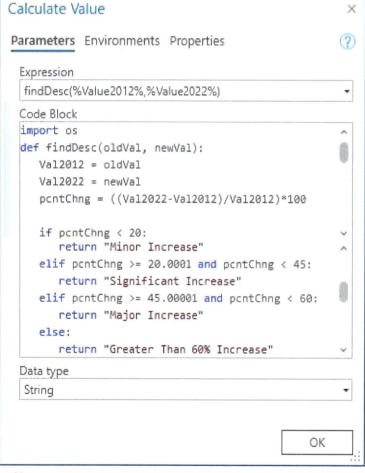

```
Calculate Value                                    ✕

Parameters  Environments  Properties              ?

Expression
findDesc(%Value2012%,%Value2022%)                 ▾

Code Block
import os
def findDesc(oldVal, newVal):
    Val2012 = oldVal
    Val2022 = newVal
    pcntChng = ((Val2022-Val2012)/Val2012)*100

    if pcntChng < 20:
        return "Minor Increase"
    elif pcntChng >= 20.0001 and pcntChng < 45:
        return "Significant Increase"
    elif pcntChng >= 45.00001 and pcntChng < 60:
        return "Major Increase"
    else:
        return "Greater Than 60% Increase"

Data type
String                                            ▾


                                          OK
```

The Expression has the name of the function and in parentheses the substitution variables from the model. By putting them in parenthesis after the function name you are passing these values into the code block.

```
Expression:

findDesc(%Value2012%,%Value2022%)
## names the function findDesc and passes in two values from the model
```

The Code Block starts with the import command to pull in the Python operating system functions.

```
Code Block:

import os
## import the Python operating system module
```

The def function is used to define the function – the name must exactly match the name you used in the Expression line. In parentheses are two new variable names that will take on the values from the Expression line, in the same order.

```
def findDesc(oldVal, newVal):
## defines the function and accepts two values
```

After the def line, everything that is part of the function should be indented three spaces.
Two variables are set to contain the values from the function definition line.

```
   Val2012 = oldVal
   Val2022 = newVal
## set two variables equal to the input values
```

A pcntChng variable is set as the calculation for percent change (see exercise 12 for details).

```
   pcntChng = ((Val2022-Val2012)/Val2012)*100
## calculate the percent change into a variable
```

An if – elif – else process is started.

```
   if pcntChng < 20:
      return "Minor Increase"
   elif pcntChng >= 20.0001 and pcntChng < 45:
      return "Significant Increase"
   elif pcntChng >= 45.00001 and pcntChng < 60:
      return "Major Increase"
   else:
      return "Greater Than 60% Increase"
## if-elif-else statement assigns categories
```

The first if statement checks for the low value.
A return command, indented three more spaces, sends back the change description text for this condition.
The elif statement checks for the second condition - value between 20.0001 and 45.
A second return command, indented three spaces, will send back a different description value.
The next elif statement checks for the next condition – value between 45.00001 and 60.
Another return command, indented three spaces, has the appropriate description value.
An else command signals the end of the if-elif-else statement and needs no condition.
The final return, indented three spaces, has the last description text.

Check your typing very carefully because Python is not very tolerant with mistakes.

3 Click OK to close the configuration window.

4 If you like, go through each tool in the model and run them individually to see if they work. Everything should be OK until you get to the Calculate Value tool, and its success will be dependent on how carefully you entered the code.

5 Save and close the model.

6 Run the model (Rafael has his fingers crossed for you).

In testing, it was taking about 90 seconds for this model to process the same dataset that the other model spent 5+ minutes on. That's a pretty good increase in speed.

As you learn more about Python and how to program with it, you will find more and more uses.

> **Rafael's Question** – *Could I just write this same code and make it into a script tool, then drop that into the model?*
> Yes – with a few modifications to the code. Plus you would have the benefit of being able to use a Python script editor which will handle the indents and other niceties for you. Any scripts that you write and make into a Script Tool will then function just like a geoprocessing tool. Earlier you saw that your models will be in the list of tools in the Geoprocessing Pane, and so will all your Python script tools.

Rafael in fact knows a lot of Python from the GIS Tutorial for Python Scripting book, so he went ahead and made a script tool out of the code from the Calculate Value tool.

1 Continue with Exercise 13.

You will notice in the Exercise13 toolbox that there is a script tool called Calculate Percent Change Script, which contains Rafael's code. First you'll look at the code and how the script tool was made, then you'll use it in the model.

2 Right click the Calculate Percent Change Script and select Edit.

This displays the Python code for this tool. If you look closely, you can see the similarity between this code and the code that was used in the Calculate Value tool.

First it imports the Python modules it needs. Then it gets two input values from the model (as integers) and uses them in a calculation. And finally it performs the If-Elif-Else routine to determine the correct category and send it back to the model.

Having the code ask for values from the model, and return values is only part of the challenge. The model has to know what the script wants and what to expect in return. This is done in the tool's configuration.

```python
## Script to calculate percent change
## and output a category
## David W. Allen, GISP  2022

## Import the Python modules
import os, string, arcpy

## Get the two values from the model
Val2012 = int(arcpy.GetParameterAsText(0))
Val2022 = int(arcpy.GetParameterAsText(1))

## Calculate the percent change
pcntChng = ((Val2022-Val2012)/Val2012)*100

## If-Elif-Else statement assigns categories
if pcntChng < 20:
    outCode = 'Minor Increase'
elif pcntChng >= 20.0001 and pcntChng < 45:
    outCode = 'Significant Increase'
elif pcntChng >= 45.0001 and pcntChng < 60:
    outCode = 'Significant Increase'
else:
    outCode = "Greater Than 60% Increase"

# Send the correct code back to the model
arcpy.SetParameter(2,outCode)
```

3 Close the Python code window.

4 Right-click the Calculate Percent Change Script again and select Properties. Click the Parameters tab.

Here you can see that the script has three parameters. The two value fields, set as Input, and one Category field, set as Output. This lets the model know to accept two input values and provide one output value.

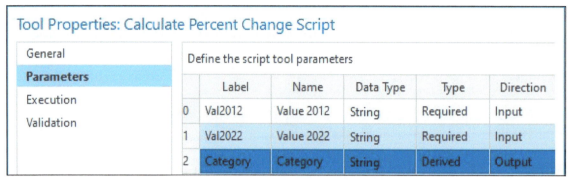

Tool Properties: Calculate Percent Change Script

		Define the script tool parameters				
General						
Parameters		Label	Name	Data Type	Type	Direction
Execution	0	Val2012	Value 2012	String	Required	Input
Validation	1	Val2022	Value 2022	String	Required	Input
	2	Category	Category	String	Derived	Output

5 Close the Tool Properties box.

6 Edit the Process Parcels for Percent Change w/Script model.

7 Drag the script tool onto the model canvas.

Notice how the tool knows to make a single output variable.

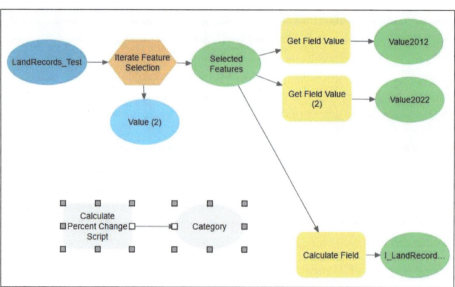

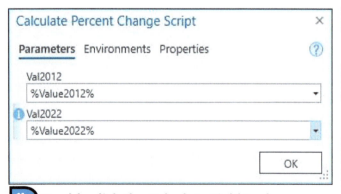

Calculate Percent Change Script   ✕

Parameters Environments Properties   ⑦

Val2012
%Value2012%   ▾

ⓘ Val2022
%Value2022%   ▾

OK

8 Double click the script tool to open it.

9 Set the two input values using variable substitution. Click OK.

10 Set the Value2012 and Value 2022 variables as preconditions of the script tool.

11 Double click the Calculate Field tool.

12 Set the Expression to Category using variable substitution. Do you think this one needs quotes?

13 Make the Category variable a precondition of the Calculate Field tool.

Save the model. Run it from the ModelBuilder menu and watch the tools as it processes the data.

There's no surprise that it does exactly what the last script did, with about the same speed. But it's another way to integrate Python scripts into your models.

> **Rafael's Question** - *It was a pain to have to re-write the Python code just to move from the Calculate Value tool to the Script tool. Isn't there a language that can transfer without changes?*
>
> Esri has developed a special scripting language called Arcade that will allow one set of code to run in desktop and web applications without modification. They are working on integrating this into the Calculate Value and script tools. Until then, brush up on your Python because it's not going anywhere.

Models and Tasks

ArcGIS Pro includes a new tool for helping to automate your processes called Tasks. These are written as tools in the Catalog Pane under a special Tasks folder, and are basically a recording of steps you might do in the ArcGIS Pro working interface. There isn't any programming involved – they don't use Python or Arcade or anything – they are just steps you take in your normal processes that you might want to record and make repeatable.

One advantage that Tasks has is the ability to record actions as you do them, and play them back. This includes interaction with the map (which models can't do). For instance, in many of your models it was required that the user select a feature or features from the map BEFORE running the model. Then you can have the model check to make sure this was done, but if not it can't then allow the user the chance to select something else without ending the model's run. With a task, however, you can turn on the Select tools and have the user do selections while the task is running. After the selections are done, the task can then check that the appropriate selections were done (like the model does) but also save the selected set for use later.

What can models do that tasks can't? Well it's a long list, starting with iterations. Tasks are a one-and-done tool and can't be set to repeat based on what's happening with the data like a model does. They also don't do calculations and define variables the way that models can. But the biggest … they can't branch or do decision making like all the Logical Branching tools in ModelBuilder.

So why use tasks? Because they can do many things that models can't AND they can call models to do the rest (just like any other geoprocessing tool).

Exercise 14 – Calling a Model with a Task

This book can't go into all the things that tasks can do, or teach you how to build all of that (but Rafael knows of a good book that can). Instead you will be given a few tasks to examine, then add a model to them that will make it more of a complete process.

1 **Start ArcGIS Pro and open Exercise 14.**

2 **In the Catalog pane, expand the tasks folder.**

3 **Right click Sample Tasks and select Edit in Designer.**

This opens the Tasks pane and the Task Designer pane. In the Tasks pane you see the lists of tasks and in the Task Designer pane you see the parameters and settings for the current task item.

4 **Click on the Select and Buffer Wells task.**

The Task Designer pane changes to show the parameters for the task itself.

5 **Right click the task and select Open.**

The begins editing the task. The Task pane shows the numbered steps in the task, and the Task Designer pane shows the parameters and settings for the steps in the task.

The first step, *1. Select Well* has already been configured. You can see that the General tab has the standard name and description.

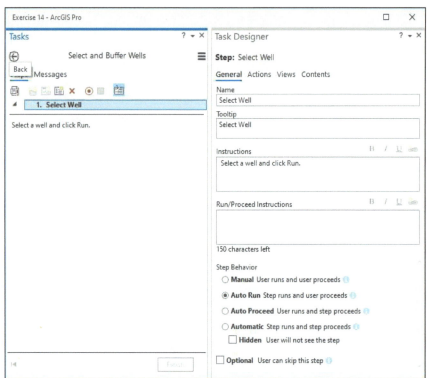

6 **Click the Actions tab in the Task Designer pane. Pause your mouse over the command line containing the word Rectangle.**

This command is what the step will execute when the task is run. It was recorded from the Edit toolbar and is the Select by Rectangle tool. It will activate the Select tool in the map window and allow the user to pick a well.

If you pause over the other icons at the right end of the line you will see that one is record, one is edit, and one is reset (erase).

7 **In the Rectangle command line, click on the Edit icon.**

Selected Command
⬚ Rectangle

Here you can more clearly see that this has the Select Features icon and the selection type of Rectangle.

Note the Type of Command line. This allows for different types of commands to be used in a task step.

8 **Click the drop down selection arrow in the Type of Command box.**

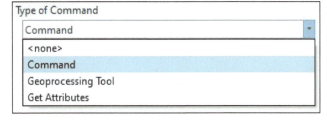

You can see the choices are Commands, which are tools picked from the active menu; Geoprocessing Tools, which are tools from the geoprocessing pane, including models; and Get Attributes, which is a way to get field values into a task (much like the Get Field Value tool inside a model).

9 **In the Task Designer click the Back arrow (don't save any changes).**

At the bottom of the Task Designer pane you will see an area for Additional Actions, with settings under the heading 'When exiting the step'. This is where the task tests that at least one well was selected before the task can move to the next step (so the model doesn't have to).

When exiting the step
Add Action ▾

Verify selection in layer Water Wells is >= 1

You will now add a step to the task that will call the model from Exercise 4 (which has been duplicated in this project, but without the Table to Excel command).

Steps   Messages

1. Sele
New Step

10 **In the Tasks pane, click the New Step icon.**

11 **In the Task Designer pane change the Name to Run the Select Parcels model.**

12 **Add a tooltip and instructions.**

13 **At the bottom of the pane, change the Step Behavior to Auto Proceed.**

The Auto Proceed choice means that the task will open a dialog and wait for the user to finish configuring a tool or interacting with the map, or whatever this step is requiring. You can see the different choices - even one that runs the step without the user even seeing it.

Task Designer   ? ▾ ✕

Step: Run the Select parcels model

General Actions Views Contents

Name
Run the Select parcels model

Tooltip
Select parcels

Instructions   B *I* U ⊸
The 'Select parcels within distance of wells' model is run.

Run/Proceed Instructions   B *I* U ⊸
Enter the required parameters and click Run.

106 characters left

Step Behavior
○ **Manual** User runs and user proceeds ⓘ
○ **Auto Run** Step runs and user proceeds ⓘ
◉ **Auto Proceed** User runs and step proceeds ⓘ
○ **Automatic** Step runs and step proceeds ⓘ
  ☐ **Hidden** User will not see the step

☐ **Optional** User can skip this step ⓘ

Next is to configure the commands that this task will execute. These are under the Actions tab. They can be configured by recording a step from the menu with your cursor but in this case you will be using a geoprocessing tool, which happens to be the model you made in Exercise 4.

These next steps go pretty deep into the settings with a lot of clicking, so follow carefully.

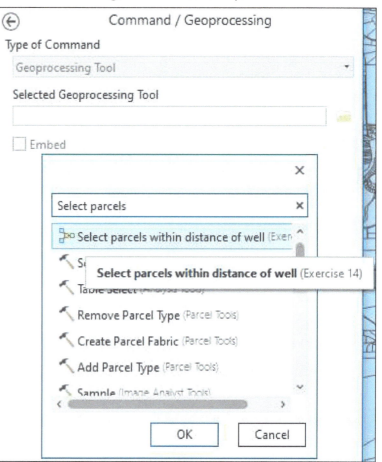

 Click the Actions tab.

 Click the Edit icon in the Command line.

16 Set the Type of Command to Geoprocessing Tool. A Selection/Search box will open.

17 Start typing 'Select parcels within ...' until you see the model appear in the listing. Select it and click OK.

You will see the parameters of the tool shown. Clicking Embed will have the model run within the dialog box of the task. You can change the default setting if you like.

18 At the bottom of the Task Designer pane click Done. You will see the actions are configured.

19 In the Tasks pane click the back arrow, then close the Tasks and Designer panes.

Rafael's Question – *When do you save the task?*
Tasks save automatically as you move from one area to another. And are saved with the project. There are ways to export a task for others to import and use.

It's time to try the task and see if it prevents the model from running with no features selected.

20 In the Catalog pane find the task and double click it.

This opens the Task Item (container for tasks). You may need to move the pane over slightly so that you can interact with the features in the map and zoom in to an area with wells and parcels.

21 Double click the Select and Buffer Wells task.

Step 1 runs and waits for you to select features in the map.

22 Move the cursor into the map and select one or more wells. Click Next Step.

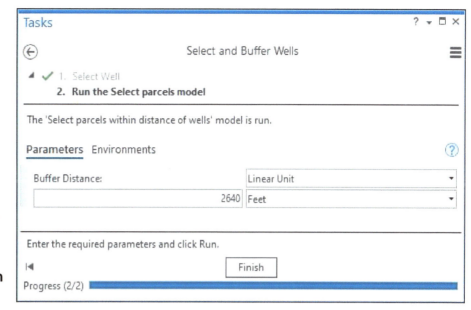

Now the model runs within the task pane and prompts for the buffer distance.

23 Use the defaults and click Finish.

Parcels within the specified distance are selected.

24 Clear all selected features, then run the task again but don't select any features - just click Next Step.

An error is raised showing the error message that was added to remind users to select features.

The task will hold on this screen until the user has selected features and clicked Next Step. This is a lot better than checking a feature selection in a model because it shows a process specific error message and gives the user a second chance to select features. The model doesn't do either of these things.

25 Select some feature and finish running the task. Then close the Tasks pane.

26 Save and close the project.

So the moral of the story is that tasks can't do what models do and models can't do what tasks do, but when they work in tandem they can produce a very powerful tool!

Rafael's Question – *Where can I learn more about tasks?*
You know that answer because GIS Guidebooks has published a tasks tutorial, filled with plenty of questions from Rafael.

Final Word

If you have completed all of the exercises and challenges in this book, you should be pretty good with models. Obviously the book can't explore every tool or give examples of every possible way to use models, but with knowledge of how these are created and configured you should be able to tackle any process!

From here, take a look at the file Rafael's Challenges in the folder where you stored the book materials. It contains several additional scenarios that you can work through on your own.

www.ingramcontent.com/pod-product-compliance
Lightning Source LLC
Chambersburg PA
CBHW042125070326
40689CB00047B/693